Anonymous

**Customs And Excise Tariff**

Anonymous

**Customs And Excise Tariff**

ISBN/EAN: 9783744758925

Printed in Europe, USA, Canada, Australia, Japan

Cover: Foto ©Suzi / pixelio.de

More available books at **www.hansebooks.com**

# CUSTOMS

### AND

# EXCISE TARIFF,

##### WITH

## LIST OF WAREHOUSING PORTS IN THE DOMINION,

STERLING EXCHANGE, FRANC, GERMAN RIXMARK, AND
THE PRINCIPAL FOREIGN CURRENCIES AT
CANADIAN CUSTOMS VALUES,

##### ALSO

A TABLE OF THE VALUE OF FRANCS IN ENGLISH MONEY.

COMPILED FROM OFFICIAL SOURCES

*Corrected to 10th June, 1882.*

### MONTREAL

MONSON, PHILLIPS & BULMER,

PUBLISHERS.

1882.

# CUSTOMS

### AND

# EXCISE TARIFF,

#### WITH

### LIST OF WAREHOUSING PORTS IN
### THE DOMINION,

**STERLING EXCHANGE, FRANC, GERMAN RIXMARK, AND
THE PRINCIPAL FOREIGN CURRENCIES AT
CANADIAN CUSTOMS VALUES,**

##### ALSO

**A TABLE OF THE VALUE OF FRANCS IN ENGLISH MONEY.**

---

#### COMPILED FROM OFFICIAL SOURCES.

*As in force from 24th February, 1882.   Corrected to 9th June, 1882.*

---

### MONTREAL:
### MORTON, PHILLIPS & BULMER,
#### PUBLISHERS.

## 1882.

# CUSTOMS TARIFF.

*As in force from 24th February, 1882.*

1.—*Resolved,* That it is expedient to provide that the value of all Bottles, Flasks, Jars, Demijohns, Carboys, Casks, Hogsheads, Pipes, Barrels, and all other vessels or Packages manufactured of Tin, Iron, Lead, Zinc, Glass, or any other material, and capable of holding Liquid ; Crates, Barrels and other Packages, containing Glass, China, Crockery or Earthenware, and all Packages in which goods are commonly placed for home consumption, including Cases in which Bottled Spirits, Wines or Malt Liquors are contained, and every package, being the first receptacle or covering, enclosing goods for purposes of sale, shall in all cases, not otherwise provided for, in which they contain goods subject to an *ad valorem* duty, be taken and held to be a part of the fair market value of such goods for duty, and when they contain goods subject to specific duty only, such Packages shall be charged with a duty of Customs of twenty per cent. *ad valorem,* to be computed upon their original cost or value ; and all or any of the above Packages described as capable of holding Liquids, when containing goods exempt from duty under this Act, shall be charged with a duty of twenty per cent. *ad valorem;* but all Packages not hereinbefore specified, and not specially charged with duty by any unrepealed enactment, and being the usual and ordinary Packages in which goods are packed for export-ation only, according to the general usage and custom of trade, shall be free of duty.

2.—*Resolved,* That it is expedient to provide that on all goods imported into Canada, subject under this Act or any other Act to *Ad valorem* duty, upon which a drawback of duties has been allowed by the Government of the country where the same were manufactured, the amount of such drawback shall in all cases be taken and considered to be a part of the fair market value of such goods and duty shall be collected thereon ; and in cases where the amount of such drawback shall have been deducted from the value of such goods upon the face of the invoice under which entry is to be made, the Collector of Customs or proper officer shall add the amount of such deduction, and collect and cause to be paid the lawful duty thereupon, and the fair market value of all goods, wares and merchandise imported into Canada, shall be understood to be the ordinary wholesale price at which the same are sold for home consumption in the country where they are purchased or manufactured without reduction of any kind because of any drawback paid or to be paid thereon, or because of any special arrangement between the seller and purchaser, having reference to the exportation of such goods, or the exclusive right to territorial limits for the sale thereof, or because of any royalty payable upon patent rights, but not payable when goods are purchased for exportation, or on account of any other consideration by which a special reduction in price might or could be obtained : Provided that nothing herein shall be understood to apply to general fluctuations of market value.

3.—*Resolved*, That it is expedient to provide that any or all of the following articles, that is to say :    Animals of all kinds, green fruit, hay, straw, bran, seeds of all kinds, vegetables (including potatoes and other roots), plants, trees and shrubs, coal and coke, salt, hops, wheat, peas and beans, barley, rye, oats, Indian corn, buckwheat, and all other grain, flour of wheat, and flour of rye, Indian meal and oatmeal, and flour or meal of any other grain, butter, cheese, fish (salted or smoked), lard, tallow, meats (fresh, salted or smoked), and lumber may be imported into Canada free of duty, or at a less rate of duty than is provided by this Act, upon proclamation of the Governor in Council, which may be issued whenever it appears to his satisfaction that similar articles from Canada may be imported into the United States free of duty, or at a rate of duty not exceeding that payable on the same under such proclamation, when imported into Canada.

4.—*Resolved*, That it is expedient to provide that if at any time any greater duty of Customs should be payable in the United States of America on tea or coffee imported from Canada than on tea or coffee imported from any other country, then the Governor in Council may impose on tea or coffee imported into Canada from the said United States, an additional duty of Customs equal to the duty payable in the United States on tea or coffee imported from Canada :    Provided that tea or coffee imported into Canada from any country other than the said United States, but passing in bond through the United States, shall be taken and rated as a direct importation from the country wherever the tea or coffee was purchased.

5.—*Resolved*, That it is expedient to provide that an allowance may be made for deterioration by natural decay or breakage upon all perishable and brittle goods imported into Canada, such as green fruits and vegetables, crockery, china, glass and glassware, provided such damage is found to exceed twenty-five per cent. of the value thereof, upon an examination to be made by an appraiser or proper officer of Customs, at the first landing, or within three days of such landing ; but such allowance shall be only for the amount of loss in excess of twenty-five per cent. of the whole quantity of such goods contained or included in any one invoice ; and provided the duty has been paid on the full value thereof, a refund of such duty may be allowed and paid in the proportion and on fulfilment of the conditions above specified, but not otherwise, on application to the Minister of Customs.

6.—*Resolved*, That it is expedient to provide that in determining the dutiable value of merchandise, except when imported from Great Britain, there shall be added to the cost the actual wholesale price or fair market value at the time of exportation in the principal markets of the country from whence the same has been imported into Canada, the cost of inland transportation, shipment and transhipment, with all the expenses included, from the place of growth, production or manufacture, whether by land or water, to the vessel in which shipment is made, either in transitu or direct to Canada.

7.—*Resolved*, That it is expedient to provide that the Governor in Council shall from time to time establish such regulations, not inconsistent with law, as may be required to secure a just, faithful and impartial appraisal of all goods, wares and merchandise imported into Canada, and just and proper entries of the

actual or fair market value thereof, and of the weights, measures or other quantities thereof, as each case may require, and such regulations, whether general or
special, so made by the Governor in Council, shall have the full force and author-
ity of law, and it shall be the duty of the appraisers of Canada and every of them,
and every person who shall act as such appraiser, or of the Collector of Customs,
as the case may be, by all reasonable ways and means in his or their power to
ascertain, estimate and appraise the true and fair market value and wholesale price,
any invoice or affidavit thereto to the contrary notwithstanding, of the merchandise at the time of exportation, and in the principal markets of the country
whence the same has been imported into Canada, and the proper weights, measures or other quantities, and the fair market value or wholesale price of every of
them as the case may require.

8.—*Resolved*, That it is expedient to provide that no refund of duty paid
shall be allowed because of any alleged inferiority or deficiency in quantity of
goods imported and entered, and which have passed into the custody of the
importer under permit of the Collector of Customs, nor because of the omission
in the invoice of any trade discount or other matter or thing which might have the
effect of reducing the value of such goods for duty, unless the same shall have
been reported to the Collector of Customs within ten days of the date of entry,
and the said goods shall have been examined by the said Collector, or by an
appraiser or other proper officer of Customs, and the proper rate or amount of
reduction certified by him after such examination, and if such Collector or proper
officer reports that the goods in question cannot be identified as those named in
the invoice and entry in question, then and in such case no refund of the duty or
any part thereof shall in any case be allowed, and all applications for refund of
duty in such cases shall be submitted with the evidence and all particulars for
decision of the Minister of Customs, who may then order payment on finding
the evidence to be sufficient and satisfactory.

9.—*Resolved*, That it is expedient to provide that the whole or part of the
duty of thirty per centum *ad valorem* imposed by this Act upon wines imported
into Canada, may be dispensed with upon proclamation of the Governor in
Council, which may be issued whenever it appears to his satisfaction that the
Governments of France and Spain, or either of them, have made changes in their
tariff of duties imposed upon articles imported from Canada in reduction or repeal
of the duties now in force in said countries.

10.—*Resolved*, That it is expedient to repeal all Acts and parts or Schedules
of Acts, and all Orders in Council imposing any duties of Customs upon goods,
wares and merchandise, or providing for the exemption of goods, wares and merchandise from Customs duty, when imported into Canada, and to make the
following provisions in lieu thereof:—

# A

P.C.

| | |
|---|---|
| Acid, Acetic............................12 cents per I.G. | |
| Acid, Muriatic........ ... .............................. | 20 |
| Acid, Nitric.................................. ........... | 20 |
| Acid, Oxalic................................................ | Free |
| Acid, Sulphuric.....................  ....½ cent per lb. | |
| Acid, Sulphuric and Nitric in a combined state........... | 20 |
| Acid, all others...................................... | 20 |
| But Carboys and Demijohns, containing, Acids, Vinegar, or other Liquids shall be subject to the same duty as if empty..................................... | 30 |
| Acetate of Lime..................................... | 20 |
| Aconite Root.......................,............... | Free |
| Account Books.................................... | 30 |
| Advertising Pamphlets ...................$1.00 per 100 | |
| Advertising Pictures, or Pictorial Show Cards, or Bills, 6 cents per lb. and................................ | 20 |
| African Teak, Wood not further manufactured than sawn or split............................................ | Free |
| Aerated Waters................................... | 20 |
| Agaric........................... ................... | Free |
| Agates, unmanufactured ............................ | Free |
| Agates, manufactured ............................... | 20 |
| Agraffe Pins of Brass, for Pianos...................... | 25 |
| Agricultural Implements, including Mower and Reaper Knives not elsewhere specified.................... | 25 |
| Agricultural Implements, parts of, not elsewhere specified, to be treated as wholes, excepting mould-boards, landsides, shares of steel, for ploughs, cut to shape, not moulded or bored, but as they come from the rollers and shears. | |
| Alabaster, Spar, Terra Cotta or Composition Ornaments... | 20 |
| Alcohol..............................$1.32½ per I.G. | |
| Ale, Beer and Porter, in Bottles (6 qts. or 12 pints to I.G.) 18 cents per I.G. | |
| Ale, Beer and Porter, in casks, or otherwise than bottles, 10 cents per I.G. | |
| Ale, Beer and Porter, barrels containing bottled ale and porter are considered packages for exportation only, and therefore free of duty........................ | Free |
| Ale, Finings........................................ | 20 |
| Ale, Ginger......................................... | 20 |
| Alkanet Root........................................ | Free |

P.C.

Almanacs, including Catalogues and Fashion Pamphlets, $1.00 per 100

| | P.C. |
|---|---|
| Almonds................................................. | 20 |
| Aloes.................................................... | Free |
| Alpacas, Wool, manufactures of, N. E. S............ .... | 20 |
| Alpaca, Hair manufactures of, not elsewhere specified..... | 20 |
| Alpaca, Hair unmanufactured.............................. | Free |
| Alum .................................................... | Free |
| Aluminium, "Chloride of," or Chloralum................. | Free |
| Aluminous Cake or Alum............................ .... | Free |
| Aluminum................................................ | Free |
| Ambergris .............................................. | Free |
| Amber, Gum............................................. | Free |
| Amber, manufactured.............................. ....... | 20 |
| Ammonia, Sulphate of................................... | Free |
| Anchors ............................................ ..... | Free |
| Anise Seed.............................................. | 20 |
| Angola, Hair unmanufactured............................ | Free |
| Angola, Hair manufactured, not otherwise specified........ | 20 |
| Annato, liquid or solid.................................. . | Free |
| Annato Seed...................... ...................... | Free |
| Annato-ine, or Extract of Annato ....................... | 20 |
| Animals, Living, of all kinds, not elsewhere specified...... | 20 |
| do    Horses, Cattle, Sheep, Swine, Dogs and pure bred Fowls, including Pheasants and Quails, for improvement of Stock under regulations to be made by the Treasury Board and approved by the Governor in Council.. | Free |

Animals brought into Canada temporarily, and for a period not exceeding three months, for the purposes of exhibition or competition for prizes offered by any agricultural or other associations. But a bond shall be first given in accordance with regulations to be prescribed by the Minister of Customs, with the condition that the full duty to which such animals would otherwise be liable shall be paid in case of their sale in Canada, or if not re-exported within the time specified in such bond.....

| Animals of all kinds, imported from Newfoundland........ | Free |
|---|---|
| Anatomical Preparations.............................. | Free |
| Aniline Dyes............................................ | Free |
| Aniline Oil, Crude...................................... | Free |
| Aniline Salts, and Arseniate of........................ | Free |
| Antelope Skins, tanned or dressed but not waxed or glazed. | 15 |
| Antelope Skins, dressed, waxed or glazed............... | 20 |
| Antimony...... ......................................... | Free |
| Antiquities, collections of ............ ................. | Free |
| Anvils................................................... | 30 |

Left margin P.C. values:

P.C.

20
20
Free

20
20

30
20
Free
30

20

Free
20
Free
Free
20
25

25

20

Free
20
20
Free

P.C.

Apparatus when imported by and for use of Colleges and Schools and Literary Societies..................... Free

Apparatus for Electric Light........................... 25

Apparel, Wearing, and other personal articles and household effects (not merchandise) of British subjects dying abroad, but domiciled in Canada.... ............. Free

Apple, dried............................2 cents per lb.

Apple, green.........................40 cents per brl.

Apple Juice, not sweetened............................ 20

Apple Juice, if sweetened, as Fruit Syrup, 1 cent per lb. and 35

Apple, Essence of ..................$1.90 per I.G. and 20

Apple Trees of all kinds....................2 cents each

Arabic Gum........................................... Free

Argols, crude........................................ Free

Argols, dust......................................... Free

Arms, including Muskets, Rifles and other fire arms, not elsewhere specified............................... 20

Arms and Munitions of War for Army and Navy and Canadian Militia................................. Free

Arrow Root........................................... 20

Artificial Flowers.................................... 25

Artificial Feathers................................... 25

Arsenic.............................................. Free

Arseniate of Aniline............................. .... Free

Articles for the use of Governor-General, Foreign Consuls General, Dominion Government, or any Departments thereof, or Senate, or House of Commons........... Free

Articles exwarehoused for Ship's Stores ................ Free

Asbestos ............................................ 20

Ashes, Pot, Pearl and Soda.......................... . Free

Asparagus........................................... 20

Asphaltum, Mineral................................... 10

Atlasses .. ......................................... 15

Australian Gum...................................... Free

Awnings and Tents................................... 25

Axes of all kinds.................................... 30

Axles of Iron or Steel (Car) .......................... 25

Axles (Carriage) .................................... 30

**B**

Babbit Metal......................................... 10

Bacon and Hams, Shoulders and Sides......2 cents per lb.

Bagatelle Tables or Boards, with cues and balls........... 35

Baggage, Travellers..... ........................... Free

Bags, Cotton, Seamless...............2 cents per lb. and 15

| P.C. | | P.C. |
|---|---|---|
| | Bags, Cotton, made up by the use of the needle ......... | 30 |
| Free | Bags, Carpet......................................... | 30 |
| 25 | Bags, Paper, printed............................. .... | 30 |
| | Bags, Paper, not printed............... ............... | 25 |
| | Bags containing fine Salt from all countries.............. | 25 |
| Free | Baking Powders...................................... | 20 |
| | Balances and Scales.......................... ..... | 30 |
| | Balls, Glass......................................... | 30 |
| 20 | Balls for Bagatelle Boards......... .................... | 35 |
| 35 | Bamboos, unmanufactured............................. | Free |
| 20 | Bamboo Reeds, not further manufactured than cut into suitable lengths for Walking Sticks, or Canes, or Sticks for | |
| Free | Umbrellas, Parasols or Sunshades.................. | Free |
| Free | Bamboos, manufactures of, not elsewhere specified........ | 25 |
| Free | Bananas............................................ | 20 |
| | Barilla............................................. | Free |
| 20 | Bark, prepared...................................... | 20 |
| | Bark, Hemlock...................................... | Free |
| Free | Bark, Oak and Tanners.............................. | Free |
| 20 | Bark, Oak, extract of, or Quercitron ................... | Free |
| 25 | Barley.............................15 cents per bushel | |
| 25 | Barley, damaged by water in transitu (on appraised value)... | 20 |
| Free | Barrels containing Bottled Ale, Beer or Porter........... | Free |
| Free | Barrels of Canadian manufacture exported filled with Domestic Petroleum and returned empty, under such | |
| | regulations as the Minister of Customs shall direct..... | Free |
| Free | Barytes, unmanufactured............................. | Free |
| Free | Barytes, manufactured............................... | 20 |
| 20 | Baskets of Willow and Bamboo....................... | 25 |
| Free | Bath Brick......................................... | 20 |
| 20 | Bay Rum..............$1.90 per I.G. and | 30 |
| 10 | Beads and Bead Ornaments........................... | 20 |
| 15 | Beans, Breadstuffs...................15 cents per bushel | |
| Free | Beans, Tonqua...................................... | 20 |
| 25 | Beans, Vanilla and Nux Vomica....................... | Free |
| 30 | Bedsteads of iron................................... | 25 |
| 25 | Bedsteads of Wood.................................. | 35 |
| 30 | Bed Feathers....................................... | 20 |
| | Beer imported in Bottles..............18 cents per I.G. | |
| | Beer imported in Wood..............10 cents per I.G. | |
| | Beef, fresh ..........................1 cent per lb. | |
| | Beef, preserved in cans....................2 cts. per lb. | |
| 10 | Bees.............................................. | Free |
| | Belladona Leaves.................................... | Free |
| 35 | Bees Wax.......................................... | 20 |
| Free | Bells for Churches.................................. | Free |
| 15 | Bells, other, as Builders' Hardware.................... | 30 |

P.C.

| | |
|---|---|
| Belts and Trusses | 25 |
| Belting of Leather | 25 |
| Belting of India Rubber | 25 |
| Benzole, not elsewhere specified........7 1/5 cents per I.G. | |
| Bent Glass, for the manufacture of Show Cases | Free |
| Berries, for dyeing or used in composing dyes | Free |
| Bibles (see Books) | 5 |
| Bichromate of Potash, crude | Free |
| Bicarbonate, or Saleratus of Potassa | 20 |
| Bicarbonate of Soda | 20 |
| Bill Heads (Books) | 30 |
| Billiard Tables, without pockets, 4½ by 9 feet or under each $22.50 and | 15 |
| Billiard Tables, without pockets, over 4½ by 9 feet, each $25.00 and | 15 |
| Billiard Tables, with pockets, 5½ by 11 feet or under, each $35.00 and | 15 |
| Billiard Tables, with pockets, all over 5½ by 11 feet, each $40.00 and | 15 |
| Binders' Cloths | 10 |
| Bird Cages, all kinds | 30 |
| Biscuits | 20 |
| Bismuth, Metallic | Free |
| Bitters (see Spirits)......$1.90 per I.G. | |
| Bitters, as Proprietary Medicines | 50 |
| Blacking, Shoe and Shoemakers', Ink, Harness and Leather Dressing | 25 |
| Black Lead | 20 |
| Black Heart Ebony Wood, not further manufactured than sawn or split | Free |
| Bladders | 20 |
| Blackberries......2 cents per quart | |
| Blanc Fixé (dry color) | Free |
| Blank Books (see Books) | 30 |
| Blankets, composed wholly or in part of Wool, Worsted, Hair of Alpaca Goat, or other like animals, 7½ cents per lb. and | 20 |
| Blue, ultramarine | Free |
| Blue (ball) | 20 |
| Blue Black (dry color) | Free |
| Boiler Plates (see Iron) | 12½ |
| Boilers and Engines, and parts of, not elsewhere specified | 25 |
| Boilers, Steam Engines and other Machinery for Ships or Sailing Vessels built in a foreign country | 25 |
| Bolts (see iron) | 30 |
| Bolts and Nuts together | 30 |

P.C.

s and Nuts for original construction of Can. Pac. Railway ... Free
ing Cloth.......................................... ..... Free
ters and Pillows.................................... 35
: Dust, for manufacture of Phosphate and Fertilizers.... Free
: Ash    "    "    "    "    "    .... Free
: Black............................................ 20
es, crude and unmanufactured, not burnt, calcined,
  ground or steamed................................ Free
es, manufactures of, not elsewhere specified.......... 20
nets, not elsewhere specified... .................... 25
ts, Printed Periodicals and Pamphlets, not elsewhere
specified, not being foreign reprints of British Copyright works, nor blank account books, nor copy books,
nor books to be written or drawn upon, nor Bibles,
prayer-books, psalm and hymn books................ 15
   Printed Periodicals :

| | |
|---|---|
| The Christian Gleaner, a monthly magazine, finished or unfinished | Free |
| The Domestic Monthly, by Blake & Co. | Free |
| Godey's Lady's Book | Free |
| Frank Leslie's Lady's Magazine | Free |
| The Ladies' Bazaar, by Leslie & Co | Free |
| Bow Bells | Free |
| The Young Ladies' Journal | Free |
| Demorest's Monthly Magazine | Free |
| La Mode Illustrée | Free |
| The Spectator, an American Review of insurance | Free |
| London Journal (a weekly) | 15 |
| Harper's Bazar | 15 |
| Demorest's Illustrated Journal | 15 |
| Frank Leslie's Pictorial | 15 |
| The World of Fashion | 15 |
| Spirit of Arkansas | 1 c. each. |
| Bazar Patterns, by J. McCall & Co | 1 c. each. |
| Metropolitan Patterns | 1 c. each. |
| Madame Demorest's Catalogue of Patterns | 1 c. each. |
| Butterick & Co's Catalogue | 1 c. each. |
| The Bazar Dress-Maker, by J. McCall & Co | 1 c. each. |
| Butterick's Metropolitan Fashions | 1 c. each. |
| Madame Demorest's Portfolio of Fashions | 1 c. each. |
| Madame Demorest's " What to Wear " | 1 c. each. |
| The Delineator, Butterick's | 1 c. each. |
| The Ladies' Quarterly Review, Butterick's | 1 c. each. |
| The Tailor's Monthly Review, Butterick's | 1 c. each. |

ks, embossed for blind. ......................... Free
ks, Bibles, Prayer-books, Psalm Books and Hymn Books   5
ks, Educational, for deaf and dumb, exclusively....... Free
ks, British Copyright works, reprint of........15% and  12½
ks, Account Books, Copy Books or books to be drawn
  or written upon................................ 30
ks, Copying Books ................................ 25
ks, printed, lithographed, or copper or steel plate bill-
  heads, cheques, envelopes and miniature newspapers,

F.C.

drafts, cards, other commercial blank forms, labels of every description and other printed matter, not elsewhere specified.................................... 30

Book Binders tools and implements...................... 10
     To include implements that are common to other trades as well as to Bookbinding, when imported by Bookbinders only, and declared by them to be for their own use, such as cutting, ruling, perforating and paging machines, ruling pens, shears, presses, binding cloth, &c.

Boots and Shoes, Leather..................... ........ 25
Boots and Shoes, Rubber............................. 25
Boots and Shoes, Felt........................... .......... 25
Boot and Shoe Counters, made from Leather Board.........
                             ½ c. per pair.

Borax .................................................. Free
Boxes, fancy ....... ..(to be rated according to material.)
Box Wood, unmanufactured............................ Free
Box Wood, manufactures of. not elsewhere specified........ 25
Botany, Specimens of................................. Free
Bottles, Glass (empty)................................ 30
Braces or Suspenders, Belts and Trusses................ 25
Brads (see Iron)....................................... 30
Bracelets, made of Hair............................... 20
Braids, all kinds. .................................... 20
Bran, Mill Feed....................................... 20
Brandy (see Spirits)....................$1.45 per I.G.
Brass, Agraffe Pins for Pianos......................... 25
Brass, old and Scrap.................................. Free
Brass, seamless drawn tubing, plain and fancy tubing...... 10
Brass, in sheets...................................... Free
Brass, Bars and Bolts.................... ................ 10
Brass Wire, round or flat.............................. 10
Brass Wire, Cloth ...................... . .............. 20
Brass, in strips, for printers' rules, not finished............... 15
Brass, in sheets, subdivisions of, such as strips, or widths cut to sizes or forms, except strips for printers' rules.......... 30
Brass Screws....................... ...................... 30
Brass Wire and Rods cut to special lengths ................. 30
Brass, manufactures of other, not elsewhere specified........ 30
Breadstuffs, other, not elsewhere specified................ 20
Brick, Building......................................... 20
Brick, Fire Brick and Tiles for lining Stoves............. 20
Brick, Bath Brick..................................... 20
Brimstone, crude or in roll or flour...................... Free
Brim Moulds, for gold beaters......................... Free
British Gum........................................... Free

| F.C. | | P.C. |
|---|---|---|
| | Bristles.............................................. | Free |
| | Bridges (see Iron)................................... | 25 |
| 30 | Britannia Metal, in pigs and bars..................... | Free |
| 10 | Britannia Metal, manufactures of, if not plated........... | 25 |
| | Britannia Metal, manufactures of, if plated.............. | 30 |
| | Bromine............................................. | Free |
| | Brooms of all kinds.................................. | 25 |
| | Broom Corn......................................... | Free |
| | Brushes............................................ | 25 |
| | Bronze or Dutch Metal............................... | 20 |
| 25 | Buck Skins (Leather) tanned or dressed, but not waxed or | |
| 25 | glazed.......................................... | 15 |
| 25 | Buck Skins (Leather) dressed, waxed or glazed.......... | 20 |
| | Buckwheat........................10 cents per bushel | |
| | Buckwheat, damaged by water in transitu (on appraised value) | 20 |
| Free | Buckwheat, meal or flour.................¼ cent per lb. | |
| | Buchu Leaves....................................... | Free |
| Free | Builders' Hardware.................................. | 30 |
| 25 | Buffalo, Bison and Camel Hair, unmanufactured.......... | Free |
| Free | "       "       "       "       manufactures of, not else- | |
| 30 | where specified....................... | 20 |
| 25 | Bulbous Roots....................................... | 20 |
| 30 | Bullion, Gold and Silver............................. | Free |
| 20 | Bullion, fringe Wool................................ | 20 |
| 20 | Bullion, fringe Silk................................. | 20 |
| 20 | Bunting (Wool) .................................... | 20 |
| | Burr Stones, in blocks, unmanufactured, not bound........ | Free |
| 25 | Burgundy Pitch..................................... | Free |
| Free | Butter...............................4 cents per lb. | |
| 10 | Buttons ........................................... | 25 |
| Free | Button Moulds...................................... | 25 |
| 10 | | |
| 10 | | |
| 20 | | |
| 15 | | |

## C

| F.C. | | P.C. |
|---|---|---|
| | Cabinet of Coins, Medals and other collections of antiquities | Free |
| 30 | Cabinet Ware or Furniture (wood)..................... | 35 |
| 30 | Cable, submarine................................... | 20 |
| 30 | Cables Chain, over 9/16 of an inch in diameter, whether | |
| 30 | shackled or swivelled or not....................... | 5 |
| 20 | Cables and Chains, all other (Iron).... ................ | 20 |
| 20 | Cachous, breath-sweeteners.............1 cent per lb. and | 35 |
| 20 | Cages, bird cages................................... | 30 |
| 20 | Calendered Paper, not ruled ......................... | 22½ |
| Free | Calf Skins, tanned or dressed, but not waxed or dressed.... | 15 |
| Free | Calf Skins, tanned or dressed, waxed or glazed.......... | 20 |
| Free | Calumba Root...................................... | Free |

P.C.

Camphor Gum........................................... 20
Canada Plates (see Iron)................. ............... 12½
Canary Seed.................... ...................... 20
Candles, Tallow........................2 cents per lb.
Candles, Paraffine Wax...................5 cents per lb.
Candles, all other, including Sperm..................... 25
Cane Juice, refined Syrups(see Sugars) ⅝ cents per lb. and 30
Cane Juice, concentrated (see sugars)...⅜ cents per lb. and 30
Canvas, for the manufacture of floor oil cloth, not less than
     45 inches wide and not pressed or calendered......... Fre
Canvas of Flax or Hemp, to be used for boat and ship sails. 5
Canvas, all other, not elsewhere specified............... 20
Cannon and Musket Powder, in kegs and barrels, 4 c. per lb.
Canister Powder, in 1 lb. and ½ lb. tins.....15 cts. per lb.
Cans, or packages made of tin or other material, con-
     taining fish of any kind, admitted free of duty under
     any existing law or treaty, not exceeding one quart in
     contents, 1½ cents per can or package ; and 1½ cents
     additional for each quartor part of.
Caoutchouc, unmanufactured.......................... Fre
Caoutchouc, Clothing................................ 30
Caoutchouc, manufactures of, not elsewhere specified....... 25
Caps, cloth, wool,..................10 cents per lb. and 25
Caps and Hats, not elsewhere specified.................. 25
Caps, Fur............................ .............. 25
Caps, Percussion, guns, rifles and pistols................ 20
Caps, Percussion Copper for blasting................... 30
Capes, Fur ......................................... 25
Cars, Railway....................................... 30
Cars, Railway and Street, the seat fixtures for, of cast iron,
     to be classed as castings........................... 25
     Locks, Hinges, Window-fasteners and similar articles,
     as also, Springs (steel) as carriage springs, to be classed
     as carriage makers' hardware...................... 30
Carbolic or Heavy Oil, used in making wooden block pave-
     ments, for treating wood for building and for railway
     ties............................................. 10
Carboys, empty or not................................ 30
Card Clothing, machine... ........................... 25
Cards, devotional.................................... 30
Cards, for playing........ ........................... 30
Cards, printed...................................... 30
Cards, Christmas and New Year chromos................ 25
Cards, embossed..................................... 25
Cards, Sunday School................................ 30
Cardamon Seed...................................... 20
Caraway Seed....................................... 20

| P.C. | | P.C. |
|---|---|---|
| 20 | Carpet Bags | 30 |
| 12½ | Carpet, treble ingrain, three-ply and two-ply carpets, composed wholly of wool.....10 cents per square yard and | 20 |
| 20 | | |
| | Carpets, two-ply and three-ply ingrain carpets, of which the warp is composed wholly of cotton or other material | |
| 25 | than wool, worsted, the hair of the Alpaca goat, or | |
| 30 | other like animal.........5 cents per square yard and | 20 |
| 30 | Carpets, Brussel | 20 |
| Free | Carpets, Dutch | 20 |
| 5 | Carpets, Jute | 20 |
| 20 | Carpets, Hemp | 20 |
| | Carpets, Tapestry | 20 |
| | Carpets, other, not elsewhere specified | 20 |
| | Cartridges, for guns, rifles and pistols | 30 |
| | Cartridges, cases | 30 |
| | Car Wheels and Axles of iron or steel | 25 |
| | Carriages, and parts of | 30 |
| | Carriages, spring (steel) | 30 |
| Free | Carriage, Railway | 30 |
| 30 | Carriage, hardware | 30 |
| 25 | Carriage, tops, frames, bodies and wheels | 30 |
| 25 | Carriage of travellers, and carriages laden with merchandise, | |
| 25 | and not to include circus troupes or hawkers, under | |
| 25 | regulations to be prescribed by the Minister of Customs, | Free |
| 20 | Carriage Dusters or Lap Wraps | 20 |
| 30 | Cashmere Shawls | 25 |
| 25 | Cashmere, of Silk | 30 |
| 30 | Cashmere, other, manufactures of, not elsewhere provided | |
| | for | 20 |
| 25 | Caskets, Burial, of any material | 35 |
| | Casts, as models for use of colleges and schools | Free |
| | Cassia, ground | 25 |
| 30 | Cassia, unground | 20 |
| | Cassimeres, wool...............7½ cents per pound and | 20 |
| | Castile and White Soap.............. 2 cents per lb. | |
| 10 | Castings, not elsewhere provided for (see Iron) | 25 |
| 30 | Castor Oil | 20 |
| 25 | Cattle, for improvement of stock | Free |
| 30 | Cattle, o' | 20 |
| 30 | Catgut Strings or Gut Cord for Musical Instruments | Free |
| 30 | Catgut or Whipgut, unmanufactured | Free |
| 25 | Celluloid Xylolite, in sheets | Free |
| 25 | Celluloid Collars | 30 |
| 30 | Cement, or in stone from quarry (13 cubic feet to ton) | |
| 20 | $1.00 per ton. | |
| 20 | Cement, burnt and unground........7½ cents per 100 lbs. | |

P.C.

Cement, Hydraulic or Waterlime, ground, including barrels,
    40 cents per barrel.
Cement, in bulk or in bags..............9 cents per bush.
Cement, Portland or Roman...........................  20
Cement, other.......................................  20
Chalk and Cliff stone, unmanufactured.................  Fre
Chalk, manufactured.................................  20
Champagne, and all other sparkling wines, in bottles, con-
    taining each not more than one quart and more than a
    pint..........................$3.00 per dozen and  30
Champagne, containing not more than a pint each and more
    than ½ pint...................$1.50 per dozen and  30
Champagne, containing ½ pint each or less........... .
    75 c. per dozen and  30
Champagne bottles containing more than one quart each
    shall pay in addition to $3.00 per dozen bottles at the
    rate of $1.50 per I.G. on the quantity in excess of one
    quart and........................................  30
    NOTE.—The quarts and pints in each case being old
    Wine Measure
Chamomile Flowers.................................  Fre
Chamois Skins......................................  20
Charts.............................................  20
Chains, Hair, Gold and Silver.....  ..................  20
Chairs, furniture, wood.............................  35
Chair (wrought Iron) for railway purposes...............  17½
Charcoal ..............................  .........  20
Cheese............................. .3 cents per lb.
Cheese Cloths................1 cent per square yard and  15
Cheques, printed...................................  30
Chemicals, not elsewhere specified.....................  20
Cherries...............................1 cent per quart
Cherries, Juice, not sweetened.......................  20
Cherries, Juice, if sweetened, as fruit syrups, 1 c. per lb. and  35
Cherry Trees....  .....................4 cents each
Chewing Gum, not sweetened.......................  20
Chewing Gum, if sweetened...........1 cent per lb. and  35
Chicory, raw or green and substituted for coffee, not else-
    where specified.....................3 cents per lb.
Chicory, dried roasted or ground, and substituted for coffee,
    composed of roots and vegetables.......4 cents per lb.
China Clay, natural or ground.........................  Fre
Chloralum or Chloride of Aluminium ..................  Fre
China Ink (as Stationery) .............................  20
China Ware.........................................  25
Chinchona Bark.....................................  Fre
Chimneys, Lamp (glass) .......................  .......  30

| P.C. | | P.C. |
|---|---|---|
| | Chloride of Lime | Free |
| | Chinese Blue | Free |
| | Chip Hats | 25 |
| 20 | Chocolate, not sweetened | 20 |
| 20 | Chocolate, containing sugar ...1 cent per lb. and | 25 |
| Free | Chronometer Clocks, as Clocks | 35 |
| 20 | Chronometer Watches | 25 |
| | Chromos, Pictures | 20 |
| | Chromos, Cards | 25 |
| 30 | Churns (wood) | 25 |
| | Church Bells | Free |
| 30 | Church Vestments | 20 |
| | Cider | 20 |
| 30 | Cigars ...60 cents per lb. and | 20 |
| | Cigarettes ...60 cents per lb. and | 20 |
| | Cinabar | Free |
| | Cinnamon Ground | 25 |
| 30 | Cinnamon unground | 20 |
| | Citrons, green fruit | 20 |
| | Citrons, rinds of, in brine for candying | Free |
| Free | Clays | Free |
| 20 | Cliff Stone, unmanufactured | Free |
| 20 | Cliff Stone, manufactured | 20 |
| 20 | Clocks, and parts of, except springs | 35 |
| 35 | Clock Springs | 10 |
| 17½ | Cloaks, Fur | 25 |
| 20 | Cloths (see Wool) ...7½ cents per lb. and | 20 |
| | Cloakings and Coatings....(see Wool) 7½ cents per lb. and | 20 |
| 15 | Clothing, Wool ...10 cents per lb. and | 25 |
| 30 | Clothing, Cotton | 30 |
| 20 | Clothing, Linen | 30 |
| | Clothing, India Rubber | 30 |
| 20 | Clothing, Silk | 30 |
| 35 | Clothing, horse clothing, shaped ...10 cents per lb. and | 25 |
| | Clothing, donation of, for charitable purposes | Free |
| 20 | Clothing, for use of army and navy and Canadian militia | Free |
| 35 | Clout Nails | 30 |
| | Coal, Anthracite, per ton ot 2000 lbs | 50 |
| | Coal, Bituminous, per ton of 2000 lbs | 60 |
| | Coal Dust, per ton of 2000 lbs | 50 |
| | Coal, other, per ton of 2000 lbs | 50 |
| Free | Coke, per ton of 2000 lbs | 50 |
| Free | Coke, Gas, when used in Canadian manufactures only | Free |
| 20 | Coal Facing | 20 |
| 25 | Coal Oil and Kerosene, distilled, purified | |
| Free | 7 1/5 cents per I.G. | |
| 30 | Coal Oil and Kerosene, fixtures and parts ther | 30 |

B

P.C

```
Coal Tar.......................................  10
Coal Pitch ...............................  10
Coats, Fur.....................................  25
Cobalt, Ore of.................................  Fr
Cocoa Matting.................................  25
Cocoanuts.........................$1.00 per 100
```

Cocoanuts, imported from place of growth by vessel direct
　　to a Canadian port.................50 cents per 100

```
Cocoa Paste and Chocolate, not sweetened..............  20
```

Cocoa Paste and other preparations of, containing sugar,
　　　　　　　　　　　　　　1 cent per lb. and  25

Cocoanut, dessicated, when sweetened....1 cent per lb. and  35

```
Cocoanut, Oil, in its natural state ...................  Fr
Cocoa Bean, shell and nibs.........................  Fr
Cod Liver Oil, medicated..........................  20
```

Cod Oil, the produce of the fisheries of the United States and
　　Newfoundland.......................................  Fr

```
Cochineal ......................................  Fr
Coffee, Green, imported from the United States...........  10
Coffee, Green, imported from other countries than U.S...  Fr
Coffee, roasted or ground, imported from U.S..3 c. p. lb. and  10
```

Coffee, roasted or ground, imported from other countries
　　than U.S..............................3 cts. per. lb.

Coffee substitutes, composed of roots or vegetables........
　　　　　　　　　　　　　　　　4 cts. per lb.

```
Coffee, all other substitutes..................3 cts. per lb.
Coffins of any materials.............................  35
Coffin Trimmings of Metal, if plated...................  30
Coins, Silver Coins from the U.S....................  20
Coins, Gold and Silver, except U.S. silver coins..........  Fr
Coir and Coir Yarn.............. ...................  Fr
Collars of linen, cotton or paper and celluloid............  30
Colchicum Seed...............................  20
Colcothar or Crocus, dry oxide of iron..................  Fr
Cologne, color in pulp............................  Fr
```

Cologne Water, and Perfumed Spirits, in bottles, flasks or
　　other packages, not weighing more than four ounces...  40

Cologne Water, and Perfumed Spirits, in bottles, flasks or
　　packages, weighing more than four ounces...........
　　　　　　　　　　　　　$1.90 per I.G. and  30

```
Colours and Paints, ground in oil or any other liquid......  25
Colours, dry, blue-black.............................  Fr
Colours, dry, blanc fixé.............................  Fr
Colours, dry, Chinese blue.........................  Fr
Colours, dry, Prussian blue and raw umber..............  Fr
```

Colours, in pulp, carmine, cologne, marjacca, rose lake,
　　scarlet and maroon, satin and fine washed white and

P.C.

| | |
|---|---|
| ultramarine blue........................................ | Free |
| olours and Paints, other, not elsewhere specified........ | 20 |
| olouring.............................................. | 20 |
| ollodion Varnish.................20 cents per I.G. and | 20 |
| oloured Sand.......................................... | 20 |
| olza Oil.............................................. | 20 |
| ombs, for dress and toilet, all kinds................... | 25 |
| ombs, curry combs, as Saddlers' hardware ............. | 30 |
| oimmercial blank forms............................... | 30 |
| ommunion Plate and plated ware for use in churches..... | Free |
| ommon Soap, brown or yellow..........1½ cents per lb | |
| ommon, soft and liquid soap, not perfumed............. | 20 |
| ommissariat Stores................................... | Free |
| omposition Nails, Spikes and Sheathing Nails........... | 20 |
| ondensed Coffee...................................... | 20 |
| ondensed Milk, not sweetened......................... | 20 |
| ondensed Milk, if sweetened.... ......1 cent per lb. and | 35 |
| onium Cicuta, or Hemlock seed and leaf............... | Free |
| onfectionery and Sugar Candy.........1 cent per lb. and | 35 |
| onfection or stick extracts (liquorice).... 1 cent per lb. and | 20 |
| ontrol Clocks, known as Watchmen's Clocks............ | 35 |
| opper bars, rods, bolts, ingots, sheets and sheathing not | |
| planished or coated............................... | 10 |
| opper, old and scrap................................. | 10 |
| opper, pigs.......................................... | 10 |
| opper, seamless drawn tubing......................... | 10 |
| opper Wire, round or flat............................ | 10 |
| opper Wire Cloth.................................... | 20 |
| opper Rivets and Burrs, and all other manufactures of, not | |
| elsewhere specified............................... | 30 |
| opy Books........................................... | 30 |
| opper, precipitate of, crude.......................... | Free |
| opper sheets, cut in strips or subdivisions.............. | 30 |
| opying Pencils....................................... | 20 |
| oral, cut or manufactured............................. | 20 |
| ord and Tassels of silk............................... | 30 |
| ordage, for ships' purposes........................... | 10 |
| ordage, other........................................ | 20 |
| ordials, as proprietary medicines...................... | 50 |
| ordials (see Spirits)......................$1.90 per I.G. | |
| orduroy................ ..........2 cts. per sq. yd. and | 15 |
| orn, Indian.....................7½ cents per bushel. | |
| orn, Indian, when damaged by water in transitu (on ap- | |
| praised value)..................................... | 20 |
| orn Meal........................40 cents per barrel | |
| orn Meal, when damaged by water in transitu (on appraised | |
| value) ............................................ | 20 |

P.C.

Cornstarch or flour (see Starch)............2 cents per lb.

Cornelians, unmanufactured...........................  Fre

Corks and Cork-wood or Cork-bark, manufactured........  20

Cork-wood or bark, unmanufactured....................  Fre

Corsets...............................................  30

Cotton Seed......................10 cents per bushel.

Cottons, grey or unbleached, bleached cotton sheetings,
    drills, ducks, cotton or Canton flannels, not stained,
    painted or printed.. ...........1 cent per sq. yd. and  15

Cottons, denims, drillings, bedtickings, cotton or Canton
    flannels, ducks or drills, dyed or coloured, checked
    and striped shirtings, cottonades, Kentucky jeans,
    pantaloon stuffs, and goods of like description.........
                        2 cents per sq. yd. and  15

Cottons over 36 inches wide, when imported by manufactur-
    ers of Window Shades for use in their factories, exclu-
    sively for the manufacture of Oiled Window Shades....  15

Cotton, duck, when to be used for boats and ships sails....  5

Cotton, all clothing made of cotton, or other material not
    otherwise provided for, including corsets, lace collars
    and similar articles made up by the seamstress or tailor,
    also, tarpaulin, plain or coated with oil, paint tar, or
    other composition, and cotton bags made up by the use
    of the needle.....................................  30

Cottons, ginghams and plaids, dyed or coloured..........
                        2 cents per sq. yd. and  15

Cotton, hosiery, shirts, drawers, woven or made on frames
    and all cotton hosiery ..........................  30

Cotton, knitted cloth................................  30

Cotton, knitting yarn, hosiery yarn, and other cotton yarn,
    under No. 40, not bleached, dyed or coloured........
                        2 cents per lb. and  15

Cotton, knitting yarn, hosiery yarn, dyed or coloured......
                        3 cents per lb. and  15

Cotton Netting for boots and shoes.................  .....  10

Cotton Parasols and Umbrellas.....................  ...  25

Cotton Prunella...................2 cents per sq. yd. an.  15

Cotton Prunella, for boots and shoes..................  10

Cotton, seamless bags...............2 cents per lb. and  15

Cotton, sewing thread, on spools......................  20

Cotton, sewing thread, in hanks, black and bleached, three
    and six cords..................................  12½

Cotton Shade...........................................  25

Cotton Velveteens and Cotton Velvets...................  20

Cotton batting, bats and warps, and carpet warps, not
    bleached, dyed or coloured.........................
                        2 cts. per lb. and  15

| P.C. | | P.C. |
|---|---|---|
| | Cotton warps on beams............1 cent per sq. yd. and | 15 |
| Free | Cotton batting, warps, dyed or coloured................. | |
| 20 | 3 cents per lb. and | 15 |
| Free | Cotton, Winceys, checked, striped and fancy, not over 25 | |
| 30 | inches wide............................................ | 20 |
| | Cottons, Winceys, checked, striped or fancy dress Wincey, over 25 inches wide and not over 30 inches, when material is not more than ¼ wool....2 c. per sq. yd. and | 15 |
| 15 | NOTE.—If over 30 inches wide and material composed partly of wool to pay..........7½ cents per lb. and | 20 |
| | Cottons, Wincey, plain, of all widths, when material is not over one-fourth wool................................ | 20 |
| | Cottons, white or dyed cotton jeans, coutilles, cambrics, | |
| 15 | silicias, casbans and printed calicos................. | 20 |
| | Cottons, all manufactures of, not elsewhere specified, held to embrace :—Quilts and sheets (white or coloured), cotton | |
| 15 | diaper, window holland, prints, printed shirtings, fur- | |
| 5 | niture prints, cretonne, plain prints, printed cotton, cashmere, cotton huckaback, cotton damask in pieces and cloths, towels, book muslin, jaconet, checked jaconet, cambric, Bishop's and Victoria lawns, tarlatans, hair cords, crinoline, and all kinds of printed muslins, leno, pique, brilliante, cotton handkerchiefs, curtains | |
| 30 | known as Swiss, Nottingham, or lace, etc., if of cotton, muslin lace, rolled jaconet, glove finished cambrics, | |
| 15 | cotton velvets and velveteens, cotton tapes, ferrets, stay-bindings, bed lace, boot web, carpet binding, blind | |
| 30 | tassels, window leno, cotton fringe, braids, boot and | |
| 30 | stay laces, and all kinds of cotton laces ............ | 20 |
| | Cotton Waste........................................ | Free |
| | Cotton Wool......................................... | Free |
| 15 | Cotton Seed Cake.................................... | Free |
| | Coutille, (cotton)................................... | 20 |
| 15 | Cranberries........................30 cents per bush. | |
| 10 | Cranks for steamboats............................... | 20 |
| 25 | Cranks for mills.................................... | 20 |
| 15 | Grapes of all kinds................................. | 20 |
| 10 | Cream of Tartar in Crystals......................... | Free |
| 15 | Crucibles .......................................... | 20 |
| 20 | Cubic Nitre......................................... | Free |
| | Cucumbers . ....................................... | 20 |
| 12¼ | Cuffs, of paper, linen or cotton..................... | 30 |
| 25 | Cummin Seed........................................ | 20 |
| 20 | Currants, green fruits.................I cent per quart | |
| | Currants, Zante and others, dried................... | 25 |
| | Curled Hair......................................... | 20 |
| 15 | Curry Combs........................................ | 30 |

Curry Cards.....................................

Cutlery, Iron and Steel, not elsewhere specified, including table, pocket and office cutlery ; scissors and shears, including sheep shears; butchers' knives and steels ; shoe, hunting, glaziers' and farriers' knives ; knives for horticultural purposes, and other articles for similar purposes as above ; horse clippers, surgical instruments, and dental instruments............................

Cutlery, if plated..............................................

Cut Flowers........................................

## D

Dates (dried fruit).................................

Debèges (woolen dress goods)............................

Decanters, and pressed or moulded table ware...............

Deer Tongue (powdered)...............................

Degras...........................................

Delaines, French.......................................

Demijohns................................ .............

Denims, cotton, dyed or colored......2 cts. per sq. yd. and

Dental instruments, wholly or in part of steel.............

Diamonds, dust or bort...............................

Diamonds, unset......................................

Dice, ivory or bone....................................

Doeskins (woolen cloth)............7 1/2 cents per lb. and

Dogs, pure bred, for improvement of stock..................

Dogs, other.............................................

Drafts, cheques and receipts..........  ................

Dragon's blood.......................................

Drain Pipes, glazed and unglazed......................

Drain Tiles, glazed and unglazed.......................

Draughts and Chessmen of ivory or bone..........  ... ..

Drawers (cotton hosiery)...............................

Drawers (wool hosiery)..............7½ cents per lb. and

Drawings and prints...................................

Drawing Slates.......................................

Drawn Tubing, copper, seamless.......................

Drawn Tubing, zinc, seamless.........................

Dressed Flag Stones.........................$1.50 per ton.

Dressed Freestone....................................

Dried Flowers........................................

Dried Roots, not elsewhere specified....................

Dried Vegetables ....................................

Drillings (cotton) dyed or colored.....2 cts. per sq. yd. and

Drills (cotton) not stained, painted or printed............

                     1 cent per sq. yd. and

| P.C. | | P.C. |
|---|---|---|
| 30 | Druggets .............................................. | 20 |
| | Drugs and Chemicals, not elsewhere specified............ | 20 |
| | Drugs, not elsewhere specified, in a crude state, used in dyeing or tanning................................ | Free |
| | Dry Putty, for polishing granite....................... | Free |
| | Dualin...............................5 cts. per lb. and | 20 |
| | Duck, for belting and hose........................... | Free |
| 20 | Duck (cottons) bleached or unbleached, not stained, painted | |
| 30 | or printed....................1 cent per sq. yd. and | 15 |
| 20 | Duck (cottons) dyed or colored.......2 cts. per sq. yd. and | 15 |
| | Duck (cottons) when to be used for boats and ships' sails. .. | 5 |
| | Duck (linen) not elsewhere specified..................... | 20 |
| | Dutch Metal or bronze............................... | 20 |
| 25 | Dust (Argol)...................................... | Free |
| 20 | Dust (bone) for manufacture of Phosphates and Fertilizers.. | Free |
| 30 | Dust, not elsewhere specified.......................... | 20 |
| 20 | Dyeing articles, in crude state, not elsewhere specified...... | Free |
| 20 | Dyes (prepared) other than Aniline.... ................. | 20 |
| 20 | Dyes, not elsewhere specified.......................... | 20 |
| 30 | Dynamite............................5 cts. per lb. and | 20 |
| 15 | | |
| 20 | | |
| Free | | |
| Free | **E** | |
| Free | Earth Closets............................,........... | 35 |
| 20 | Earth, Fuller's, prepared.......................... ...... | 20 |
| 20 | Earth, Fuller's, not prepared.......................... | Free |
| Free | Earthenware, stoneware and white granite, or iron stoneware | |
| 20 | and C.C. ware, whether decorated, printed or sponged | |
| 30 | or not.......................................... | 30 |
| Free | Earthenware and stoneware, brown or colored, and Rock- | |
| 20 | inghara ware..................................... | 25 |
| 20 | Earthenware and Crockery, not elsewhere specified........ | 20 |
| 20 | Ebony, not further manufactured than sawn or split........ | Free |
| 30 | Edge Tools, not elsewhere specified.................... | 30 |
| 20 | Eggs .............................................. | Free |
| 20 | Egg boxes, when imported from the United States to be | |
| 25 | filled with eggs and exported, may be returned to Cana- | |
| 10 | da to be refilled without requiring duty a second time, | |
| 10 | but duty must be paid on first importation............ | 25 |
| | Elastic Web ......................................... | 25 |
| 20 | Electric and Galvanic Batteries ........................ | 25 |
| 20 | Electric Lights, apparatus for......... ................. | 25 |
| 20 | Electro-plated Ware, not classed as jewelry.............. | 30 |
| 20 | Electrotypes and Stereotypes, for commercial blanks and | |
| 15 | advertisements.................................. | 20 |
| | Electrotypes and stereotypes of standard books........... | 10 |
| 15 | Embossed Books, for the blind....................... | Free |

P.C

| | |
|---|---|
| Embossed Cards, not business or advertising | 25 |
| Embroideries, not otherwise provided for | 20 |
| Emery | Fr |
| Emery Cloth | 25 |
| Emery Paper | 25 |
| Emery Wheels | 25 |
| Engines, Locomotives | 25 |
| Engines, Fire | 25 |
| Engines, all others, and boilers | 25 |
| Engravings and Prints | 20 |
| Entomology, specimens of | Fr |
| Envelopes, paper of all kinds, not printed | 25 |
| Envelopes, printed | 30 |
| Ergot | Fr |
| Esparto, or Spanish Grass, for the manufacture of paper | Fr |
| Essences of Apple, Pear, Pine Apple, etc. $1.90 per I.G. and | 20 |
| Essences, mixed with spirits $1.90 per I.G. and | 20 |
| Essences, such as Essence of Old Tom, Scotch whisky, etc. | 20 |
| Essential or Volatile Oils, for manufacturing purposes | 20 |
| Excelsior, for Upholsterers' use | 20 |
| Extracts, containing spirits $1.90 per I.G. and | 20 |
| Extract of Logwood | Fr |
| Extract of Malt, for medicinal purposes | 25 |
| Extract of Meat | 20 |
| Extract of Sumac | 20 |
| Evergreens | 20 |

## F

| | |
|---|---|
| Fancy boxes, ornamental cases, rated according to material. | |
| Fans, Advertising | 30 |
| Fans, all others | 25 |
| Farina 2 cts. per lb. | |
| Fashion Pamphlets $1.00 per 100 | |
| Feathers, Ostrich and Vulture, undressed | 15 |
| Feathers, Ostrich and Vulture, dressed | 25 |
| Feathers, for beds | 20 |
| Feathers, Artificial, not elsewhere specified | 25 |
| Felloes, spokes, hubs and parts of wheels, rough, hewn or sawn only | 15 |
| Felt, for boots and shoes, when imported by manufacturers for use in their factories | 15 |
| Felt, for glove lining, when imported by manufacturers for use in their factories | 10 |
| Felt, endless, for paper makers, when imported by manufacturers for use in their factories | 10 |

P.C.      P.C.

| | | |
|---|---|---|
| 25 | lt, (pull over) for hats | 25 |
| 20 | lt, adhesive, for sheathing vessels | Free |
| Fr | lt, for skirts, when imported by the manufacturers for use | |
| 25 | in their factories | 15 |
| 25 | lt, Roofing | 20 |
| 25 | lt Cloth, of every description, not elsewhere specified.... | |
| 25 | 7½ cts. per lb. and | 20 |
| 25 | lt Boots and Shoes | 25 |
| 25 | lt, other, not elsewhere specified | 20 |
| 20 | lt Hats | 25 |
| Fr | bre, Mexican | Free |
| 25 | bre, Tampico | Free |
| 30 | bre, vegetable, for manufacturing purposes | Free |
| Fr | brilla and Istle | Free |
| Fr | gs | 25 |
| | lberts | 20 |
| 20 | les | 30 |
| 20 | llets, of Cotton and Rubber, not exceeding 7 inches wide, | |
| 20 | for manufacture of card clothing | Free |
| 20 | nger Bars, railway (iron) | 17½ |
| 20 | ngering Yarn, under No. 30........7½ cts. per lb. and | 20 |
| 20 | re-arms, muskets, rifles, pistols and shot guns | 20 |
| Fr | re-arms, for use of army, navy and Canada militia | Free |
| 25 | re-brick or Tiles, for lining stoves and furnaces | 20 |
| 20 | re Clay | Free |
| 20 | re Engines | 25 |
| 20 | re Extinguishers (chemical) | 25 |
| | re-proof Paint, dry....................¼ cent per lb. | |
| | re Works | 25 |
| | sh, fresh, salted or smoked, except free by Washington | |
| | Treaty...............1 cent per lb. | |
| 30 | sh, of all kinds, the produce of the fisheries of the United | |
| 25 | States, except fish of the Inland Lakes, or of rivers falling into them, and fish preserved in oil | Free |
| 15 | sh-bait | Free |
| 25 | sh, fresh and salted or smoked, from Newfoundland | Free |
| 20 | sh Oil, and products of fish, from Newfoundland | Free |
| 25 | sh, preserved in oil | 20 |
| | sh Oil, produce of the fisheries | Free |
| 15 | sh hooks, nets, seines, lines and twines, for the use of the fisheries, but not to include sporting fishing tackle, or | |
| 15 | hooks with flies, or trawling spoons | Free |
| | shing Rods | 30 |
| 10 | sh Plates, steel (see steel rails) | Free |
| | sh Plates, iron | 17½ |
| 10 | sh Plates, for use of Canada Pacific Railway | Free |

P.(

Flannels, of every description, not elsewhere specified (wool)
7½ cts. per lb. and    20

Flasks, "glass" of every description .....  ............  .    30

Flax, fibre, scutched......................1 cent per lb.

Flax, fibre, hackled......................2 cents per lb.

Flax, tow of, scutched or green.............½ cent per lb.

Flax Seed............................10 cents per bush.

Flax Seed Oil....................................  ..    25

Flax Twine, Sail Twine..............................     5

Flax Twine, other.......................................    25

Flax, manufactures of, not elsewhere specified.............    20

Flint, flints and ground flint stones......................    Fr

Flour, Wheat...................  ..........50 cts. per bbl.

Flour, Buckwheat or Meal................1/4 cent per lb.

Flour, of Corn or Corn Meal.............40 cents per bbl.

Flour of Rye.....  ....................50 cents per bbl.

Flour of Rice.............................2 cents per lb.

Flour of Sago............................2 cents per lb.

Flour, Grain and Meal of all kinds, when damaged by water
in transitu (on appraised value) ....................    20

Flowers, artificial, not elsewhere specified........... ....    25

Flower Seeds, when in bulk or in large packages..........    15

Flower Seeds, when put up in small papers or parcels......    25

Fog Signals, detonating for railway alarms..............    20

Folia Digitalis.. .....................  .............    Fr

Food, Milk, manufactured by Henri Nestle, Dr. Gibaut and
others, and all other similar preparations.............    30

Forgings, iron, not elsewhere specified................. ...    25

Forks, hay, manure and potatoe, of steel................    30

Fossils ..............................................    Fr

Fowls, pure bred, also pheasants and quails for improvement of stock.....................................    Fr

Fowls, other.......................................................    20

French or Flower Odors, imported in tins of not less than 10
lbs. each..........................................    15

French Mustard........................................    25

Fringes and other trimmings, not elsewhere specified......    20

Frogs, railway, iron..................................    17

Frog points, railway, iron.........  .................    17

Fruits, dried, Apples.....................2 cents per lb.

Fruits, dried, Currants, Dates, Figs, Plums, Prunes, Raisins
and all others, not elsewhere specified..............    25

Fruit, green, Apples....................40 cts. per bbl.

Fruits, green, Blackberies, Gooseberries, Raspberries and
Strawberries.........................2 cts. per qt.

Fruits green, Cherries and Currants..........1 ct. per qt.

P.C.                                                                      P.C.

ruits, green, Cranberries, Plums and Quinces...........
20                                    30 cts. per bush.
30   ruits, green, Grapes..................... 2 cts. per lb.
ruits, green, Lemons................................   20
ruits, green, Oranges...............................   20
ruit, green, Peaches..................40 cts. per bush.
ruits, green, other, not elsewhere specified ..............   20
25   ruit, in air-tight cans, including cans, if sweetened.......
5                                          3 cts per lb.
25   ruit, in air-tight cans, including cans, if not sweetened....
20                                      2 cts. per lb.
Free      The rate to include the duty on the cans and the weight
          on which duty shall be payable, to include the weight
          of the cans.
ruits, preserved in brandy and other spirits. .$1.90 per I.G.
ruit Jars and Preserve Jars, glass ......................   30
uller's Earth........................................   Free
uller's Earth, prepared...............................   20
urniture, house, cabinet or office, finished or in parts......   35
20   ur Skins, of all kinds, not dressed in any manner........   Free
25   ur Skins, wholly or partially dressed......................   15
15   ur hats, caps, muffs, tippets, capes,  coats,  cloaks and
25       other manufactures of fur.......  .............  ....   25
20   use......  .......................................   20
Free

30
25
30                            **G**
Free  aiters, woolen clothing .............. 10 cts. per lb. and   25
      alateas, cottons................... 2 cts. per sq. yd. and   15
Free  alvanized Nails and Spikes, wrought and pressed ........
                                    ¾ ct. per lb. and   10
20   alvanic Batteries..................................   25
     arden Seeds, when in bulk or in large parcels............   15
15   as and Coal Oil Fixtures, or parts thereof..............   30
25   as Coke, when used in Canadian manufactures only.......   Free
20   as Light Shades....................................   30
17½  as Pipes of cast iron.................................   25
17½  as, for dentists and others.............................   20
     asaliers...........................................   30
     elatine, and all similar preparations...................   20
25   entian Root.......................................   Free
     erman and Nickel Silver, manufactures of, not plated .....   25
     erman and Nickel Silver, plated ......................   30
     erman and Nickel Silver, in sheets...................   10
     iant Powder........................5 cts. per lb. and   20
     ilt Ware, of all kinds................................   30

P.C

| | |
|---|---|
| Gin (Spirits).........................$1.32½ per I.G. | |
| Gin (Old Tom).......................$1.32½ per I.G. | |
| Ginger Ale.......................................... | 20 |
| Ginger and Spices, of all kinds, except Mace and Nutmegs, unground ......................................... | 20 |
| Ginger and Spices, of all kinds, ground.................. | 25 |
| Gingham, cotton..................2 cts. per sq. yd. and | 15 |
| Ginseng Root...................................... | Fr |
| Girondoles and Gasaliers............................. | 30 |
| Glass, Ornamental, Figured, Enamelled Sand and stained... | 30 |
| Glass, Carboys and Demijohns, Bottles and Decanters, Flasks and Phials of every description, Telegraph and Lightning Rod Insulators, Jars and Glass Balls, and pressed or moulded Table Ware............................ | 30 |
| Glass, Lamp and Gas-light Shades, Lamps and Lamp Chimneys, Globes for Lanterns, Lamps and Gas Lights..... | 30 |
| Glass, stained, tinted or painted........................ | 30 |
| Glass, window, stained .............................. | 30 |
| Glass, common and colorless window glass.............. | 30 |
|     Imitation porcelain shades and colored glass, not figured, painted, enameled or engraved.............. | 20 |
| Glass, figured, enameled and obscured white............... | 30 |
| Glass Stoppers......... ...................... ...... | 20 |
| Glass, all other, and manufactures of, not elsewhere specified ............................................. | 20 |
| Glass and Emery Paper............................... | 25 |
| Glass, Plate, silvered................................ | 30 |
| Glass, Plate, not silvered............................. | 20 |
| Glazier's knives (cutlery) not plated ................... | 20 |
| Glengarry or Scotch Caps............................. | 25 |
| Globes, geographical, when imported by and for use in colleges and schools................................. | Fr |
| Globes, stationery ................................... | 20 |
| Gloves, cotton and lisle and thread.................... | 25 |
| Gloves, silk........................................ | 25 |
| Gloves and Mits, of cotton, leather, silk, woolen, or any other material.................................. | 25 |
| Glue .............................................. | 20 |
| Glucose Syrup.....................½ cent per lb. and | 35 |
| Glucose and Grape Sugar, to be classed and rated for duty as sugar, according to grade, by Dutch Standard. | |
| Glycerine........................................... | 20 |
| Goat Hair, unmanufactured............................ | Fr |
| Gold Beaters' moulds and skins........................ | Fr |
| Gold Laces, Knots, Stars, &c.......................... | 20 |
| Gold and Silver Ware, plated, and Electro-plated Ware...... | 30 |
| Gold and Silver Cloth................................ | 20 |

P.C.                                                                    P.C.

old and Silver Jewelry.............................. 20

old and Silver leaf................................. 25

20  old and Silver, manufactures of, not elsewhere specified... 20

20  rain, of all kinds, when damaged by water in transitu (on
      appraised value) ............................... 20

25  ranite, all manufactures of, not elsewhere specified....... 20

15  rapes, green fruit........................2 cts. per lb.

Fre rape Vines of all kinds ............................. 20

30  rass, Manilla and Sea Grass........................,............ Free

30  rass, manufactures of................................ 20

    ravels............................................. Free

    rease and Grease Scrap, for manufacture of soap........ Free

    rease and Grease Scrap, except for manufacture of soap... 20

30  rease, Axle........................................ 20

    rease, Foot, the refuse of the cotton seed after the oil is
30      pressed out..................................... Free

30  rease, other....................................... 20

30  rindstones.............................$2.00 per ton.

30  round or pulverized saw dust....................... 25

    uano, and other animal and vegetable manure, not phos-
20      phate........................................... Free

30  ums, Amber, Arabic, Australian, British, Dextrine, Copal,

20      Damar, Mastic, Sandarac, Shellac and Tragacanth.... Free

    ums, Assafœtida, Camphor, Opium and others, not else-
20      where specified................................. 20

25  ums, chewing, sweetened.............1 cent per lb. and 35

30  ums, chewing, not sweetened. ..................... 20

20  um, shellac, bleached and drawn..................... 20

20  unpowder, gun, rifle and sporting, in kegs, ½ kegs and ¾

25      kegs, and similar packages.............5 cts. per lb.

    unpowder, cannon and musket, in kegs and bbls........

Fre                                              4 cts per lb.

20  unpowder, canister, 1 lb. and ½ lb. tins....15 cts. per lb.

25  unpowder, blasting and mining............3 cts. per lb.

25  un, rifle and pistol cartridges and cartridge cases........ 30

    ut and Worm Gut, manufactured or unmanufactured, for
25      whip and other cord............................. Free

20  utta Percha, manufactures of, not elsewhere provided for 25

35  utta Percha clothing, except when partly composed of
      wool ........................................... 30

    utta Percha clothing, when partly composed of wool......
20                                    .       10 cts. per lb. and 25

Fre utta Percha, crude................................... Free

Fre ypsum, crude (Sulphate of Lime)..................... Free

20  ypsum, ground and calcined......................... 20

30  ypsum or Plaster of Paris, ground not calcined..........

20                                    10 cts. per 100 lbs.

# H

P. C

| | |
|---|---|
| Hair, Alpaca, Angola, Bison, Buffalo, Camel, Goat, Hog, Horse and Human, not curled or otherwise manufactured | Fr |
| Hair, Cow, Calf and Deer, in the natural state | Fr |
| Hair, curled | 20 |
| Hair Cloth and Seating Cloth | 20 |
| Hair Mattresses | 35 |
| Hair Oils, Pomatums and Pastes, and all other perfumed preparations used for the hair, mouth and skin | 30 |
| Hams, fresh, salted, dried or smoked ........ 2 cts. per lb. | |
| Hammocks | 25 |
| Handkerchiefs, cotton and linen | 20 |
| Handkerchiefs, Silk | 30 |
| Hangings, paper or wall paper | 30 |
| Hardware, builders', cabinet-makers', upholsterers', carriage makers', saddlers' and undertaker's | 30 |
| Hardware, other | 20 |
| Harness, dressing | 25 |
| Harness and saddlery | 25 |
| Hats, caps and bonnets, not elsewhere specified | 25 |
| Hatters' plush, of silk or cotton | 10 |
| Hatters' furs, not on the skin | Fr |
| Hay and Straw | 20 |
| Hay Forks, steel | 30 |
| Head Lights, glass | 30 |
| Heavy Oil or Carbolic Oil | 10 |
| Hemlock Bark | Fr |
| Hemlock, seed and leaf | Fr |
| Hemp, undressed | Fr |
| Hemp, Indian, (crude drug) | Fr |
| Hemp Rags, fit only for manufacture of paper | Fr |
| Hemp, Twine | 25 |
| Hemp, other manufactures of, not elsewhere specified | 20 |
| Henbane, leaf | Fr |
| Hickory, lumber unmanufactured | Fr |
| Hides, raw, whether dry, salted or pickled | Fr |
| Hinges and Locks | 30 |
| Hoes, steel | 30 |
| Hollow-ware, tinned, glazed or enamelled, of cast or wrought iron | 25 |
| Holly | 20 |
| Hominy | 20 |
| Honey, in the comb or otherwise ........... 3 cts. per lb. | |

P.C.

oofs, horns and horn tips............................. Free
oop Iron, thicker than 17 gauge...................... 17½
oop Iron, 17 gauge or thinner........................ 12½
ops.....................................6 cts. per lb.
orn and Ivory, manufactures of........................ 20
orn Strips, used in making corsets.................... Free
orned Cattle, for improvement of stock.............…..... Free
orned Cattle, not elsewhere specified..................... 20
orse Clothing, shaped (woolen)........10 cts. per lb. and 25
orse Clippers, cutlery................................ 20
orse Shoes........................................... 30
orse Shoe Nails...................................... 30
orses, not elsewhere specified ........................ 20
orses, for improvement of stock...................... Free
ose, rubber.......................................... 25
osiery of Cotton, not elsewhere specified.............. 30
osiery of silk....................................... 30
osiery, wool of all kinds, not elsewhere specified........
7½ cts. per lb. and 20
ubs, spokes, felloes and parts of wheels, roughly hewn or
sawn only........................................ 15
ubs, spokes, felloes and parts of wheels, when finished... 25
ydraulic Cement or White Lime, ground, including bbl...
40 cts. per bbl.
ymn Books........................................... 5
yoscyamus Leaves..................................... Free
yoscyamus Seed.......................................…... 20

**I**

e.................................................... Free
cense................................................ 20
dian Corn..........................7½ cts per bush.
dian Corn Meal.....................40 cts. per bbl.
dian Hemp, crude drug................................ Free
dia Rubber, boots and Shoes, and manufactures of, not
elsewhere specified............................... 25
dia Rubber Clothing................................... 30
dia Rubber, unmanufactured........................... Free
digo................................................ Free
digo, extract of..................................... 20
k, for writing....................................... 25
k, for printing...................................... 20
k Powder............................................ 20
kstands, except electro-plated........................ 20
sect Powder......................................... 20
inglass.............................................. 20

P.(

| | |
|---|---|
| Instruments, Philosophical, for the use of colleges | Fɪ |
| Instruments, Musical, for bands, for the use of army and Navy and Canadian Militia | Fɪ |
| Insulators, telegraph and lightning rods | 30 |
| Ipecacuanha Root | Fɪ |
| Iris Root | Fɪ |
| Iron Sand, for polishing granite | Fɪ |
| Iron, Agricultural Implements, not elsewhere specified | 25 |
| Anvils | 30 |
| Band and Hoop Iron, No. 17 guage or thinner | 12 |
| Band and Hoop Iron, thicker than 17 guage | 17 |
| Bars, rolled or hammered, including flats, rounds and squares | 17 |
| Bars, other, in slabs, blooms, loops, etc | 10 |
| Boiler Plate | 12 |
| Bolts, washers and rivets | 30 |
| Bedsteads and other iron furniture and ornamental iron work | 25 |
| Canada plates | 12 |
| Car Wheels and Axles, of iron or steel | 25 |
| Castings and Forgings of every description, not elsewhere specified | 25 |
| Cast Iron, Gas, Water, and Soil Pipes | 25 |
| Chain Cables, over 9/16 of an inch in diameter, whether shackled or swivelled or not | 5 |
| Chain and Cables, all other | 20 |
| Cultivators and Ploughs | 25 |
| Engines, Locomotive | 25 |
| Engines, Fire | 25 |
| Engines, other and boilers | 25 |
| Fire Extinguisher (chemical) | 25 |
| Hardware, viz., builders', cabinet makers', upholsterer's, carriage makers', saddlers' and undertakers' | 30 |
| Hardware, not elsewhere specified | 20 |
| Hollow-ware, tinned, glazed or enamelled | 25 |
| Horse Shoe and Horse Shoe Nails | 30 |
| Iron Bridges and structural iron work | 25 |
| Iron Masts, for ships or parts of | Fɪ |
| Iron, not otherwise provided for | 17½ |
| Locks, of all kinds | 30 |
| Machines, Sewing $2 each and | 20 |
| Mowing and Reaping Machines | 25 |
| Threshing Machines | 25 |
| Middlings Purifier | 25 |
| Other machinery, composed wholly or in part of iron, not elsewhere specified | 25 |
| Malleable Iron Castings | 25 |

P.C.
Fr

| | P.C. |
|---|---|
| Mill Iron and Mill Cranks, and Wrought Forgings for Mills and Locomotives, or parts thereof, weighing 25 lbs. or more | 20 |
| Nail and Spike Rods | 17½ |
| Nails, Hungarian and Clout | 30 |
| Nails, Iron Wire, Pointe de Paris | 30 |
| Nails, Spike and Sheathing Nails, composition | 20 |
| Nails and Spikes, wrought and pressed, including Railroad Spikes ¾ ct. per lb. and | 10 |
| Nails and Spikes, cut 1/2 ct. per lb. and | 10 |
| Nuts of iron or steel 1 ct. per lb. and | 10 |
| Nuts and Bolts, together | 30 |
| Old and Scrap Iron $1.00 per ton. | |
| Pig Iron, Charcoal $2.00 per ton. | |
| Pig Iron, all other $2.00 per ton. | |
| Railway Bars or Iron Rails for Railways or Tramways | 15 |
| Railway Fish Plates, Frogs, Frog Points, Chairs and Finger Bars | 17½ |
| Rolled beams, channel and angle and T iron, steel or iron and steel | 12½ |
| Rolled, round wire rods in coils, under 1/2 inch diameter | 10 |
| Safes, and doors for safes and vaults | 25 |
| Screws, iron and steel, commonly called "wood screws" | 35 |
| Scales, balances and weighing beams | 30 |
| Sheet Iron, smoothed or polished, coated or galvanized and common or black, No. 17 gauge and thinner. | 12½ |
| Sheet Iron, common, thicker than No. 17 gauge | 17½ |
| Skates, iron or steel | 30 |
| Stoves | 25 |
| Tacks, brads and sprigs | 30 |
| Tin Plates | Free |
| Tubing, lap-welded boiler iron tubing, not threaded, coupled or otherwise manufactured, 1½ inch in diameter and over | 15 |
| Wrought Iron tubing, plain, not threaded, coupled or otherwise manufactured, over 2 in. in diameter... | 15 |
| Wrought Iron Tubing, plain, 2 in. in diameter or under, coupled and threaded or not | 25 |
| Wrought Iron Tubing, other than above | 20 |
| Wire, iron and steel | 15 |
| Wire Rope, strand or chain made of iron wire | 25 |
| Wire Work, other | 25 |
| Manufactures of Iron, all other, not otherwise proded for | 20 |
| le or Tampico "fibre" | Free |
| ry Nuts, unmanufactured | Free |

C

## L

| | |
|---|---|
| 'els of every description, printed, lithographed. or copper or steel plate...... | 30 |
| Dye, crude, seed, button, stick and shell...... | Free |
| es, cotton...... | 20 |
| es, embroidered with gold and silver...... | 20 |
| es, silk...... | 20 |
| e Collars, clothing...... | 30 |
| kers, Varnish, not elsewhere specified...... | |
| 20 cts. per I.G. and | 20 |
| :es, scarlet and maroon, in pulp...... | Free |
| np Black...... | 20 |
| ıb and Sheep Skins, tanned or dressed, but not waxed or glazed...... | 15 |
| ıb and Sheep Skins, dressed, waxed or glazed...... | 20 |
| np Reflectors...... | 30 |
| nps (Glass)...... | 30 |
| np Shades, glass...... | 30 |
| ı-welded Boiler Iron Tubing, not threaded, coupled or otherwise manufactured, 1½ inch in diameter and over. | 15 |
| d, tried or rendered......2 cts. per lb. | |
| d, untried......1 1/2 cts. per lb. | |
| d Oil...... | 20 |
| a, unmanufactured...... | Free |
| a, manufactures of...... | 20 |
| d, bars, blocks and sheets......60 cts. per 100 lbs. | |
| d, old, scrap and pig......40 cts. per 100 lbs. | |
| d, white and red, dry, and orange mineral, also dry white zinc...... | 5 |
| d, white, in pulp, not mixed with oil...... | 5 |
| d pipe and shot...... | 30 |
| d pencils, in wood or otherwise...... | 25 |
| d, all manufactures, not elsewhere specified...... | 30 |
| ther, all upper and French Kid, tanned but not waxed.. | 15 |
| ther, all upper and French Kid, dressed and waxed.... | 20 |
| ther Belting and Gloves and Mitts...... | 25 |
| ther Boots and Shoes...... | 25 |
| ther Board......3 cts. per lb. | |
| ther Boot and Shoe Counters, made from leather board... 1/2 ct per pair. | |
| ther, Cordova, tanned, from horse hide, and manufactures of...... | 25 |
| ther, Morocco skins, tanned but rough or undressed.... | 10 |
| ther, other, and skins tanned, not elsewhere specified... | 20 |

P.C.

Leather, Patent, Japanned or enamelled................... 2c
Leather, Sole, tanned but rough or undressed............. 10
Leather, Sole and Belting Leather, tanned but not waxed.. 15
Leather, Sole and Belting Leather, dressed and waxed..... 20
Leather, manufactures of, not elsewhere specified........... 25
Leeches............................................. Free
Leicester and Lincolnshire or Lustre Wools, such as are
    grown in Canada.......................3 cts. per lb.
Lemons, citrons and oranges, in brine for candying........ Free
Lemons and Oranges................................. 20
Lentils .............................................. 20
Lignumvitæ wood, not manufactured ................... Free
Lime and Lemon Juice................................... 20
Lime Juice, containing spirits..............$1.90 per I.G.
Lime Juice, sweetened, as confectionery.... 1 ct, per lb. and 35
Lime, Acetate of.................................... 20
Lime................................................. 20
Lime, Chloride of ................................... Free
Linen collars and cuffs (clothing)...................... 30
Linen Clothing, or articles worn by men, women and
    children ......................................... 30
Linen, Duck.......................................... 20
Linen Canvas, when to be used for boats and ships sails.... 5
Linen, manufactures of, not elsewhere specified........... 20
Linen Thread ........................................ 20
Lines and Twines, for the fisheries ..................... Free
Linings, rolled, (cotton).............................. 20
Linoleum, as Oil Cloth................................ 30
Linseed Oil, raw or boiled ........................... 25
Liquorice, root and paste, extract of, for manufacturing pur-
    poses............................................ 20
Liquorice Root and Rhubarb Root, natural state.......... Free
Liquorice, stick extract or confection......1 ct. per lb. and 20
Litharge............................................. Free
Lithographic Stones, not engraved...................... 20
Litmus and all Lichens, prepared and not prepared........ Free
Lobsters, fresh or preserved from the U. S. Fisheries ...... Free
Lobsters, fresh or preserved, other than from U. S. Fish-
    eries............................................. 20
Locks, of all kinds.................................. 30
Locomotives, and Railway Passenger, Baggage and Freight
    Cars, being the property of railway Companies in the
    United States running upon any Line of Road crossing
    the Frontier, so long as Canadian Locomotives and Cars
    are admitted free under similar circumstances into the
    United States, under regulations to be prescribed by the
    Minister of Customs.............................. Free

| P.C. | | P.C. |
|---|---|---|
| 20 | Locomotive Engines.................................. | 25 |
| 10 | Locomotive Tires of steel or "Bessemer," in the rough..... | 10 |
| 15 | Locomotive wrought forgings, or parts thereof, weighing 25 | |
| 20 | lbs. or more..................................... | 20 |
| 25 | Logwood, extract of................................ | Free |
| Free | Logs, and round unmanufactured timber, not elsewhere | |
| | provided for.................................. | Free |
| | Lubricating Oils, all kinds ......................... | 25 |
| Free | Lumber and Timber, Planks and Boards, sawn, of Boxwood, | |
| 20 | Cherry, Walnut, Chestnut, Mahogany, Pitch Pine, | |
| 20 | Rosewood, Sandal-wood, Spanish Cedar, Oak, Hickory | |
| Free | and Whitewood, not shaped, planed or otherwise manu- | |
| 20 | factured........................................ | Free |
| | Lumber and Timber, Spanish Cedar cut by knife.......... | Free |
| 35 | Lumber and Timber, not elsewhere specified.............. | 20 |
| 20 | | |
| 20 | **M** | |
| Free | | |
| 30 | Mace.............................................. | 25 |
| | Macaroni and Vermicelli............................. | 20 |
| 30 | Machine Card Clothing.............................. | 25 |
| 20 | Machine, Dating.................................... | 25 |
| 5 | Machine, Knitting .................................. | 25 |
| 20 | Machine, Numbering................................. | 25 |
| 20 | Machine, Sewing, whole or on heads or parts of heads...... | |
| Free | $2 each and | 20 |
| 20 | Machine, Sewing, parts of; stands and table tops imported | |
| 30 | separately, stands to be treated as castings and wood | |
| 25 | work as manufactures of wood...................... | 25 |
| | Machine Screws, except Wood Screws.................. | 30 |
| 20 | Machine Screws, intended for holding in wood, without | |
| Free | nuts or other iron fixtures, to be classed as wood screws | 35 |
| 20 | The same imported with nuts, or properly screw bolts. | 30 |
| Free | Machines, Ruling, Cutting, Perforating and Paging Machines, | |
| 20 | as Bookbinders' Implements.......................... | 10 |
| Free | Machinery, not elsewhere mentioned.................... | 25 |
| Free | Madder, or Indian Madder, ground and prepared, and all | |
| | extracts of...................................... | Free |
| 20 | Mackerel, fresh, from U. S. fisheries ................... | Free |
| 30 | Mackerel, fresh, other, not elsewhere specified........... | |
| | 1 ct. per lb. | |
| | Mackerel, pickled, from U. S. fisheries ................. | Free |
| | Mackerel, pickled, other, not elsewhere specified......... | |
| | 1 ct. per lb. | |
| | Magnesia .......................................... | 20 |
| | Mahogany, lumber, sawn, not shaped, planed or otherwise | |
| Free | manufactured.................................... | Free |

P.C

| | |
|---|---|
| Majolica Ware, Stone Pottery ........................ | 30 |
| Malleable Iron Castings............................. | 25 |
| Malt, upon entry for Warehouse, subject to Excise Regulations...........................15 cts. per bush. | |
| Malt, extract of, for medicinal purposes ................ | 25 |
| Manilla Grass........................................ | Fr |
| Mantels, Slate and Marble........................... | 30 |
| Mantles, clothing, wool...............10 cts. per lb. and | 25 |
| Mantles, clothing, other, not elsewhere specified.......... | 30 |
| Manures, Guano, and other animal and vegetable manures... | Fr |
| Maps............................................... | 20 |
| Marble Dust........................................ | 20 |
| Marble Blocks, from the quarry, in the rough, or sawn on two sides only, and not specially shapen, containing 15 cubic feet or over..................................... | 10 |
| Marble Blocks and Slabs, sawn on more than two sides....... | 20 |
| Marble Slabs, sawn on not more than two sides .......... | 15 |
| Marble, manufactures of, not elsewhere specified .......... | 30 |
| Marbles (playing marbles)............................. | 20 |
| Mastic Gum......................................... | Fr |
| Masts, Iron for ships, or parts of...................... | Fr |
| Matches, of wax.................................... | 20 |
| Matches, of wood.................................... | 25 |
| Material for Bridges, being for original construction of Canadian Pacific Railway .............................. | Fr |
| Mathematical and Philosophical Instruments, not elsewhere specified........................................... | 20 |
| Mattresses, hair, spring and other ..................... | 35 |
| Matting, Cocoa...................................... | 25 |
| Matting and Mats, not elsewhere specified............... | 20 |
| Meal, when damaged by water *in transitu* (on appraised value) | 20 |
| Meal, Buckwheat........................¼ ct. per lb. | |
| Meal Cake, Oil Cake, Cotton Seed Cake, and Palm Nut Cakes | Fr |
| Meal, Indian Cornmeal ...................40 cts. per brl. | |
| Meats, Bacon and Hams, Shoulders and sides...2 cts. per lb. | |
| Meats, Beef, fresh or salted....................1 ct. per lb. | |
| Meats, Beef, Corned Beef....................2 cts. per lb. | |
| Meats, Beef, imported in the carcase to be cured or preserved in bond for exportation......................1 ct. per lb. | |
| Meats, Extract of .................................. | 20 |
| Meats, Mutton, fresh or salted................1 ct. per lb. | |
| Meats, Pork ...............................1 ct. per lb. | |
| Meats, Pork, imported, to be cured in bond....1 ct. per lb. | |
| Meats, Poultry, and Game of all kinds .................. | 20 |
| Meats, prepared meats, sealed or unsealed, in cans or otherwise, not elsewhere specified.................2 cts. per lb. | |
| Meats, other, not elsewhere specified .........2 cts. per lb. | |

P.C.

Medals of gold, silver or copper.................................... Free

Medicines, Proprietary, viz.: all tinctures, pills, powders,
troches or lozenges, syrups, cordials, bitters, anodynes,
tonics, plasters, liniments, salves, ointments, pastes,
drops, waters, essences, oil or medicinal preparations
or compositions recommended to the public under any
general name or titles, as specifics for any diseases or af-
fections whatsoever, affecting the human or animal
bodies, not elsewhere provided for, in liquid form....   50

Medicines, Patent, all other, not elsewhere specified........   25

Meerschaum, crude or raw .............................. Free

Meerschaum, manufactures of..........................   20

Melado...................................⅜ per lb. and   30

Melons]........................................................   20

Menageries, horses, cattle, carriages and harness of, under
regulations to be prescribed by the Minister of Customs   Free

Mercury or quicksilver..................................... Free

Metal Composition, not elsewhere specified..................   20

Metal, yellow Metal in bars, bolts and for sheathing.......... Free

Mexican Fibre............................................. Free

Mica ......................................................   20

Military Store and munitions of war....................... Free

Milk Food manufactured by Henri Nestle, Dr. Gibaut, and
others, and all other similar preparations ..................   30

Mill board; not straw board ..............................   10

Mill Iron and Mill Cranks, and wrought forgings for Mills
and Locomotives, or parts thereof, weighing 25 lbs. or
more ......................................................   20

Millinery, to be rated according to material of chief value.... 

Mineral and Aërated Waters...............................   20

Mineral and Bituminous substances not elsewhere specified..   20

Mineralogy, specimens of .................................. Free

Mitts and Gloves, of kid and leather ......................   25

Mitts and Gloves, all other...............................   25

Models and Patterns of Inventions and other Improvements
in the Arts, but no articles shall be deemed as models or
improvements which can be fitted for use.............   Free

Mohair, manufacture, not elsewhere specified .............   20

Molassess, if used for refining, or clarifying purposes, or
for the manufacture of sugar, when imported from the
country of growth or production ..................   25
Including Export duty and other Government taxes.

Molasses for same purpose as above, and not imported direct
from country of growth and production .............   30
Export duty and other Government tax included.

Molasses, when not so used and imported direct from the
country of growth and production, including Export

| | P.C. |
|---|---|
| duty and other Government Tax ...................... | 15 |
| Molasses when not so used, and not imported direct from country of growth and production, including Export duty and other Government tax...................... | 20 |
| Moleskin, pantaloon stuff.................2 cts. per yd. and | 15 |
| Morphine........................................... | 20 |
| Morroco Skins, tanned, but rough or undressed ............. | 10 |
| Moss, Iceland, and other Mosses, crude................... | Free |
| Moss, Seaweed, and all other vegetable substances used for beds and mattresses, in their natural state, or only cleaned.......................................... | Free |
| Moss, other ...................................... | 20 |
| Moulds, Button..................................... | 25 |
| Mowing and Reaping Machines........................ | 25 |
| Mowers and Reapers' Knives and Cutter Bars, as edged tools.......................................... | 30 |
| Mucilage, as stationery.............................. | 20 |
| Muffs, Fur......................................... | 25 |
| Munjeet, or Indian Madder, ground or prepared, and all extracts of......................................... | Free |
| Muriatic Acid ...................................... | 20 |
| Muriate of Potash, crude,............................. | Free |
| Muslin, printed, (see other cottons) ...................... | 20 |
| Music, printed sheet music ...................6 cts. per lb. | |
| Musical Instruments for bands of the Army and Navy....... | Free |
| Musical Instruments, not elsewhere specified.............. | 25 |
| Muskets, Rifles, Guns and Pistols, not elsewhere specified... | 20 |
| Musk, in pods, or in grains........................... | Free |
| Mustard Cake ...................................... | 20 |
| Mustard Seed, unground............................. | 15 |
| Mustard, prepared, including French Mustard............. | 25 |

# N

| | |
|---|---|
| Nails and Spike Rods (iron)........................... | 17½ |
| Nails, Hungarian and Clout........................... | 30 |
| Nails, Iron Wire, Pointe de Paris ...................... | 30 |
| Nails, Spikes and Sheathing, Nail Composition........... | 20 |
| Nails and Spikes, wrought and pressed, including R.R. Spikes...............................¾ ct. per lb. and | 10 |
| Nails and Spikes, cut..................1/2 ct. per lb. and | 10 |
| Napkin Rings, not plated............................. | 20 |
| Napkin Rings, if plated.............................. | 30 |
| Naptha, not elsewhere specified..........7 1/5 cts. per I.G. | |
| Neatsfoot Oil, and all animal oils, not elsewhere specified... | 20 |
| Needles, Knitting, and all other......................... | 20 |

P.C.

ettings, Cotton and Woolen Nettings for boots, shoes and
   Gloves........................................... 10
ets and Seines, for use of fisheries........................... Free
ewspapers and quarterly, monthly and semi-monthly Maga-
   zines, unbound............................................. Free
ewspapers and quarterly, monthly and semi-monthly maga-
   zines, if bound........................................... 15
ew Year Chromos or embossed cards........................ 25
ickel................................................... Free
ickel and German Silver, in sheets........................ 10
ickel and German Silver, manufactures of, not plated....... 25
ickel and German Silver, manufactures of, if plated ....... 30
itrate of Saltpetre..................................... 20
itrate of Soda......................................... Free
itric Acid ........................................... 20
itro-Glycerine......................10 cts. per lb. and 20
otarial Seals......................................... 20
umbering Machine, not to be classed with printing presses,
   to pay................................................. 25
uts and Bolts, together (iron) ........................... 30
uts, iron and steel.....................1 ct. per lb. and 10
uts, all kinds (dried fruits)............................. 20
uts, Cocoa, imported from place of growth direct to a
   Canadian port.......................50 cts. per 100
uts, Cocoa, not imported direct...........$1.00 per 100
ut, Cocoa and Palm Oil, in their natural state........... Free
utmegs and Mace..................................... 25
utgalls.............................................. Free

## O

ak and Tanners' Bark................................. Free
ak, lumber and timber, not further manufactured than
   sawn or split......................................... Free
akum ................................................ Free
ats....................................10 cts. per bush.
ats, damaged by water in transitu (on appraised value).... 20
atmeal.................................1/2 ct. per lb.
atmeal, damaged by water in transitu (on appraised value) 20
chres, dry, ground or unground, washed or unwashed, not
   calcined.............................................. 10
chres, calcined....................................... 20
il, Aniline, crude.................................... Free
il, Coal and Kerosene, distilled, purified or refined, Naptha,
   Benzole and Petroleum............7 1/5 cts. per I.G.
il, Carbolic, defined as the product of coal tar, in a crude
   state................................................. 10

P.C

Oil, Castor............................................ 20
Oil, Cod Liver, medicated............................. 20
Oils, Cocoanut and Palm, in their natural state............ Fr
Oil, Cod.............................................. Fr
Oils, Fish, and products of fish, from Newfoundland....... Fr
Oils, Fish, the product of the U. S. fisheries............. Fr
Oil, Flax Seed or Linseed................................ 25
Oil, Hair, perfumed or not............................... 30
Oil, Lard Oil........................................... 20
Oil, Lubricating, of all kinds............................ 25
Oils, Neatsfoot and all animal ..... ..................... 20
Oil, Olive............................................. 20
Oil, product of Petroleum............... .......7 1/5 per I.G.
Oil, Seal, the product of U.S. fisheries or Newfoundland.... Fr
Oil, Salad............................................. 20
Oil, Sesame seed....................................... 20
Oil, Sperm............................................ 20
Oils, Vegetable Oils, not elsewhere specified.............. 20
Oils, Volatile or Essential.............................. 20
Oils, Whale, or fish from Newfoundland ................. Fr
Oil, all other, not elsewhere specified.................... 20
Oil, Whale, in casks from on shipboard, and in the condition
     in which it was first landed......................... Fr
Oil Cake, Cotton Seed Cake, Palm Nut Cake and Meal.... Fr
Oil Cloths in the piece, cut or shaped, oiled, enamelled,
     stamped, painted or printed, flocked or coated, includ-
     ing Linoleum...................................... 30
Oil Cloths, for table covers, carriages, etc................ 30
Old and Scrap Copper.................................. 10
Old and Scrap Iron.............$1.00 per ton of 2000 lbs.
Old and Scrap Lead...............40 cts. per 100 lbs.
Opium (drug).......................................... 20
Opium, prepared for smoking...................$5 per lb.
Oranges, rinds of, in brine for candying.................. Fr
Oranges, green fruits .................................. 20
Ornamental Cases (to be rated according to material).
Ores of Metal, of all kinds............................. Fr
Organs, Cabinet Reed Organs, having not more than two
     sets of reeds..........................each $10 and   15
Organs, etc., having over two and not over four sets of reeds,
                                       each $15 and   15
Organs, etc., having over four and not over six sets of reeds
                                       each $20 and   15
Organs, etc., having over six sets of reeds.....each $30 and   15
Organs, sets or parts of sets of reeds for Cabinet Organs.... 25
Organs, Pipe Organs ................................... 25
Ornamental, figured and enamelled Plate Glass........... 30

P.C.

Ornamental Iron Work............................... 25
Ornaments for Ladies' Head Dresses, Hats, Bonnets, Belts,
  Dress Clasps, etc., to be rated according to the material
  component part of chief value.
Orris Root....................................... Free
Ostrich Feathers, undressed...................... 15
Ostrich Feathers, dressed........................ 25
Osiers, unmanufactured........................... Free
Osiers and Willow Furniture...................... 35
Osiers and Willow Works, not elsewhere specified......... 25
Oxalic Acid...................................... Free
Oysters, fresh in shell.......................... Free
Oysters, in cans, fresh, the product of U. S. Fisheries........ Free
Oysters, in cans, fresh, other................... 20
Oysters, preserved, other than United States............. 20
Oysters, shelled, in bulk, product of the U.S............. Free

## P

Packages—"See 1st item of Resolutions."
Pails, Tubs and Churns, wood..................... 25
Paints and Colors, dry, viz., blue black, blanc fixé, Chinese
  blue, Prussian blue and raw umber................. Free
Paints and Colors, colors in pulp, viz., carmine, cologne,
  marjacca and rose lakes, scarlet and maroon, satin and
  fine washed white and ultramarine blue.............. Free
Paints and Colors, viz., fire-proof paint, dry.... $\frac{1}{4}$ ct. per lb.
Paints and Colors, ground in oil or in any other liquid..... 25
Paints and Colors, Ochres, dry, ground or unground, washed
  or unwashed, not calcined....................... 10
Paints and Colors, Paris Green, dry.............. 10
Paints and Colors, White and Red Lead and Orange Min-
  eral........................................... 5
Paints and Colors, White Lead in pulp, not mixed with oil. 5
Paints and Colors, Zinc, dry white............... 5
Paints and Colors, dry, other, not elsewhere specified........ 20
Paintings, engravings, Drawings and Prints........ 20
Paintings in Oil or Water Colors, by artists of well-known
  merit, or copies of old masters by such artists.......... Free
Palm Leaf, unmanufactured....................... Free
Palm Leaf, when manufactured.................... 20
Palm Nut, Cake and Meal......................... Free
Palm Oil (natural state)......................... Free
Pamphlets, N.E.S................................. 15
Pamphlets, Advertising.....................$1.00 per 100
Pamphlets, Fashion.........................$1.00 per 100

P.C

| | |
|---|---|
| Paper Collars, Cuffs and Shirt Fronts of paper, linen or cotton...... | 30 |
| Paper Bags, not printed...... | 25 |
| Paper Bags, if printed ...... | 30 |
| Paper, Cards, for playing ...... | 30 |
| Paper Hangings, including window shades and trunk linings | 30 |
| Papier Maché, manufactures of...... | 25 |
| Paper, Carpet Lining...... | 20 |
| Paper, Mill board, not Straw board...... | 10 |
| Paper, of all kinds, not elsewhere specified...... | 20 |
| Paper, Printing...... | 20 |
| Paper, ruled...... | 25 |
| Paper, Union Collar Cloth, not shapen...... | 10 |
| Paper, waste or clippings...... | Free |
| Paper, manufactures of, including cornices, edgings, etc., for cigar boxes, perforated or embossed paper, confectionery paper, book marks, tags, card and cardboard, photographic mats, etc...... | 25 |
| Paper, Sand Paper...... | 25 |
| Paper, calendered, including writing and note paper, not ruled ...... | 22½ |
| In its meaning held practically to apply to all writing papers, smooth surface papers, whether colored or white, drawing paper and enamelled paper, but does not apply to ordinary printing paper, known to the trade as "news" paper, or to wrapping, tissue, filtering paper, which latter are...... | 20 |
| Paper binders or fasteners, as stationery...... | 20 |
| Paper Weights and Clips, as stationery...... | 20 |
| Paraffine Wax, or Stearine......3 cts. per lb. | |
| Paraffine Wax Candles ......5 cts. per lb. | 24 |
| Parasols and Umbrellas, all kinds...... | 25 |
| Parts of Pianos...... | 25 |
| Paste, Cocoa, containing Sugar......1 ct. per lb. and | 25 |
| Paste, Cocoa, not sweetened...... | 20 |
| Paste, perfumed...... | 30 |
| Patent Medicines, in liquid form (see medicines)...... | 50 |
| Patent Medicines, other than liquid...... | 25 |
| Patent Leather...... | 20 |
| Peaches, green fruit ......40 cts. per bush. | |
| Pears, green fruit...... | 20 |
| Pear, essence of......$1.90 per I.G. and | 20 |
| Pear Trees......4 cts. each | |
| Peas......10 cts. per bush. | |
| Peas, when damaged by water in transitu (on appraised value) | 20 |
| Pearl, Mother of, not manufactured...... | Free |
| Pearl, manufactures of...... | 20 |

P.C.

| | |
|---|---|
| ncils, Lead, in wood or otherwise............................. | 25 |
| ncils, Slate............................................ | 20 |
| ncil Cases............................................. | 20 |
| ns................................................... | 20 |
| nholders.............................................. | 20 |
| nknives............................................... | 20 |
| lts................................................... | Free |
| pper, unground......................................... | 20 |
| pper, ground........................................... | 25 |
| rcussion Caps, for guns, rifles........................... | 20 |
| rcussion Caps, for blasting.............................. | 30 |
| riodicals, Illustrated Advertising (see posters)........... | |
| 6 cts. per lb. and | 20 |
| riodicals, N.E.S....................................... | 15 |
| rfumery, including toilet preparations.................... | 30 |
| rfumed Spirits in bottles or Flasks, not weighing more than four ounces...................................... | 40 |
| rfumed Spirits in bottles, flasks or other packages, weighing more than 4 oz...............$1.90 per I.G. and | 30 |
| rfumed and Fancy Soaps................................. | 30 |
| rsis, or extract of Archill and Cudbear.................. | Free |
| troleum, refined................7 1/5 cts. per I.G. | |
| troleum, products of................7 1/5 cts. per I.G. | |
| wter, Platina or Metal Composition...................... | 20 |
| easants, for improvement of stock....................... | Free |
| easants, other........................................ | 20 |
| ials, glass............................................ | 30 |
| ilandri Seed........................................... | 20 |
| ilosophical Instruments and Apparatus, including globes and pictorial illustrations of insects, when imported by or for the use of colleges and schools, scientific and literary societies...................................... | Free |
| ilosophical and Mathematical Instruments, other......... | 20 |
| osphorus.............................................. | Free |
| osphor Bronze blocks, sheets and wire.................... | 10 |
| anofortes, square, whether round-cornered or not, not over 7 octaves........................$25 each and | 15 |
| anofortes, square, all other................$30 each and | 15 |
| anofortes, upright........................$30 each and | 15 |
| anofortes, concert, semi-concert. or parlor grand pianoforte...............................$50 each and | 15 |
| anos, part of.......................................... | 25 |

A piano imported, consisting of case, frame, soundingboard, etc., but without the action, should be treated as a piano liable to the specific duty and the *ad valorem* duty on its value in that state.

| | |
|---|---|
| ckles and Sauces...................................... | 20 |

|  | P.C. |
|---|---|
| Pictorial Show Cards.....................6 cts. per lb. and | 20 |
| Picture Frames.................................................... | 35 |
| Picture Advertising .............................................. | 30 |
| Pictures, N.E.S.................................................... | 20 |
| Pig, Copper....................................................... | 10 |
| Pig Iron.........................$2 per ton of 2000 lbs. | |
| Pig Tin............................................................ | Free |
| Pig Zinc .......................................................... | Free |
| Pillows and Bolsters............................................. | 35 |
| Pimento, ground.................................................. | 25 |
| Pimento, unground............................................... | 20 |
| Pins, hooks and eyes ............................................ | 20 |
| Pine Apple........................................................ | 20 |
| Pine Apple, essence of...............$1.90 per I.G. and | 20 |
| Pipe, Clay........................................................ | Free |
| Pipes, drain pipes and sewer pipes ............................ | 20 |
| Pipes, soil and water pipes, of iron castings................. | 25 |
| Pipes, Tobacco pipes............................................ | 20 |
| Pipe Organs...................................................... | 25 |
| Pistols........................................................... | 20 |
| Pitch-pine ....................................................... | Free |
| Pitch, Coal....................................................... | 10 |
| Plants and Shrubs, lawn and ornamental trees, not elsewhere specified...................................................... | 20 |
| Plants, viz.: | |
|     Apple Trees, of all kinds.......................2 cts. each. | |
|     Cherry Trees, of all kinds....................4 cts. each. | |
|     Peach Trees................................................. | 20 |
|     Pear Trees, of all kinds.......................4 cts. each. | |
|     Plum Trees, of all kinds.......................5 cts. each. | |
|     Quince Trees...................................2 1/2 cts. each. | |
| Plaster of Paris or Gypsum, ground not calcined............... 10 cts. per 100 lbs. | |
| Plaster of Paris, calcined or manufactured.................... 15 cts. per 100 lbs. | |
| Plaits, Straw, Tuscan and Grass................................ | Free |
| Plated Ware and Gilt Ware, of all kinds, including cutlery, plated wholly or in part........................................ | 30 |
| Plates, Canada ................................................... | 12½ |
| Plate, Boiler..................................................... | 12½ |
| Plates, Tin....................................................... | Free |
| Plate Glass, not silvered....................................... | 20 |
| Plate Glass, if silvered ........................................ | 30 |
| Platina, not elsewhere specified................................ | 20 |
| Plates, engraved on wood, steel or other metal................ | 20 |
| Playing Cards ................................................... | 30 |
| Plums, green fruits.....................30 cts. per bush. | |

| P.C. | | P.C. |
|---|---|---|
| 20 | lums, dried fruits | 25 |
| 35 | lum Trees .... 5 cts. each. | |
| 30 | lumbago | 10 |
| 20 | lumbago, manufactures of | 20 |
| 10 | lush, Silk Netting, used for manufactures of gloves | 15 |
| | lush, of Silk or Cotton, for Hatters' use | 10 |
| Free | lush Silks, other | 30 |
| Free | olishing Powders | 20 |
| 35 | omades, french or flower odors, preserved in fat or oil for | |
| 25 | the purpose of conserving the odors of flowers which | |
| 20 | do not bear the heat of distillation when imported in | |
| 20 | tins of not less than 10 lbs. each | 15 |
| 20 | omades, all other | 30 |
| 20 | omatum, or paste for the hair, mouth or skin | 30 |
| Free | orcelain Slate | 25 |
| 20 | orcelain Ware, other | 25 |
| 25 | ork .... 1 cent per lb. | |
| 20 | orter, in bottles .... 18 cts. per I.G. | |
| 25 | orter, in wood .... 10 cts. per I.G. | |
| 20 | ortland or Roman Cement | 20 |
| Free | osters and advertising pamphlets or pictorial show cards or | |
| 10 | bills .... 6 cts. per lb. and | 20 |
| 20 | otash, bichromate of, crude | Free |
| | otash, muriate of, crude | Free |
| | Potatoes, sweet | 20 |
| | otatoes, other .... 10 cts. per bush. | |
| 20 | Poultry and Game of all kinds | 20 |
| | owder, rifle and sporting powder .... 5 cts. per lb. | |
| | Blasting and Mining powders .... 3 cts. per lb. | |
| | Cannon and Musket .... 4 cts. per lb. | |
| | Canister powder .... 15 cts. per lb. | |
| | Giant, Dualin, Dynamite .... 5 cts. per lb, and | 20 |
| | Nitro Glycerine .... 10 cts. per lb. and | 20 |
| | owders, perfumed | 30 |
| Free | owders, Baking | 20 |
| | Prayer Books (see books) | 5 |
| 30 | roprietary Medicines, in liquid form (see medicines) | 50 |
| 12½ | recipitate of copper, crude | Free |
| 12½ | rints, drawings, etc. | 20 |
| Free | rinting Presses, not to include type writers, electric pens, | |
| 20 | numbering machines or dating stamps | 10 |
| 30 | runes and Plums, dried fruit | 25 |
| 20 | runella, twill cotton .... 2 cts. per sq. yd. and | 15 |
| 20 | runella, cotton and woolen netting for boots and shoes | 10 |
| 30 | russian Blue, dry color | Free |
| | umice and Pumice Stone, not ground or powdered | Free |

P.C.

Pumice Stone, ground or powdered........................ 20
Putty.................................................... 25
Putty, dry, for polishing granite.......................... Free

# Q

Quails, for improvement of stock......................... Free
Quails, other............................................ 20
Quercitron, or extract of oak bark........................ Free
Quills................................................... 20
Quicksilver.............................................. Free
Quinces ..............................30 cts. per bush.
Quince Trees........................2 1/2 cts. each.
Quinine, sulphate of (in powder)......................... Free

# R

Rags, of cotton, linen, jute, hemp, paper, waste or clippings
    and waste of any kind fit for manufacturing paper....... Free
Rags, woolen............................................ Free
Rails, iron or railway bars, for railway or tramway. ........ 15
Railway Iron, fish plates, frogs, frog points, chairs and fin-
    ger bars............................................ 17½
Railway Bars and Fish Plates, steel, until the close of the
    Session of Parliament next ensuing the passing of this
    Act, unless sooner repealed ......................... Free
Railway Cars and Railway Carriages................·....... 30
Raisins, dried fruits...................................... 25
Rakes, steel............................................. 30
Rakes, Teeth, steel...................................... 30
Rasps, steel............................................. 30
Raspberries, green fruit ......................2 cts. per qt.
Rattans, unmanufactured ................................ Free
Rattans, manufactured or partly manufactured.............. 20
Receipts, printed........................................ 30
Reeds, unmanufactured ................................. Free
Reeds, manufactured or partly manufactured .............. 20
Reeds, for organs ....................................... 25
Rennet, raw or prepared ................................ Free
Revolvers, not elsewhere specified ....................... 20
Rhubarb Root........................................... Free
Ribbons, of all kinds and material ....................... 30
Rice, unhulled or paddy, when imported direct trom the
    country of growth or production ..................... 17½
Rice, other.................................1 ct. per lb.
Rice Flour.................................2 cts. per lb.
Ridges Food............................................. 20

P.C.

| P.C. | | P.C. |
|---|---|---|
| | Rifles, not elsewhere specified | 20 |
| 20 | Rifle Cartridges | 30 |
| 25 | Kinds of lemons, citrons and oranges, in brine for candying | Free |
| Free | Rivets, Bolts and Washers | 30 |
| | Rosin | Free |
| | Roofing Felts | 20 |
| | Rockingham Ware | 25 |
| Free | Roofing and other Tiles | 20 |
| 20 | Rolled Beams, channel and angle T iron and steel, or iron | |
| Free | and steel | 12½ |
| 20 | Rolled Round Wire Rod in coils (iron) under 1/2 inch in | |
| Free | diameter | 10 |
| | Rope Iron Wire | 25 |
| | Rope, other, as cordage | 20 |
| Free | Roofing Slate, black or blue............80 cts. per sq. | |
| | Roofing Slate, red, green or other.............$1 per sq. | |
| | Roots, medicinal, viz.: Aconite, Calumba, Ipecacuanha, | |
| | Sarsparilla, Squills, Terraxicum and Valerian | Free |
| | Rose Lake (color in pulp) | Free |
| Free | Rose Water, without spirits | 30 |
| Free | Rose Wood Lumber, not further manufactured than split or | |
| 15 | sawn | Free |
| | Rubber, unmanufactured | Free |
| 17½ | Rubber Clothing of cotton and rubber | 30 |
| | Rubber (Tweed) Clothing.............10 cts. per lb. and | 25 |
| | Rubber, other manufactures of | 25 |
| Free | Ruling Pens | 10 |
| 30 | Rum.................. . $1.32 1/2 per I.G. | |
| 25 | Rum Shrub.............$1.90 per I.G. | |
| 30 | Russel Cord Wool | 20 |
| 30 | Rye.................10 cts. per bush. | |
| 30 | Rye, damaged by water in transitu (on appraised value) | 20 |
| | Rye Flour .............50 cts. per barrel. | |
| Free | Rye Flour, when damaged by water in transitu (on appraised | |
| 20 | value | 20 |
| 30 | | |
| Free | **S** | |
| 20 | | |
| 25 | Saddlers' Hardware | 30 |
| Free | Saddlers' Soap | 20 |
| 20 | Safes, iron, and doors for safes and vaults | 25 |
| Free | Saffron Cake | Free |
| 30 | Saffron and Safflower, and extract of | Free |
| | Sago | 20 |
| 17½ | Sago Flour .............2 cts. per lb. | |
| | Sails for boats and ships | 25 |
| | Sail Twine | 5 |
| 20 | **D** | |

|  | P. |
|---|---|
| Sal-Ammonia............................................... | Fr |
| Sal-Soda................................................. | Fr |
| Saleratus, or Bicarbonate .............................. | 20 |
| Salt imported from the United Kingdom or any British possession, or imported for the use of the sea or gulf fisheries, not otherwise provided for ...................... | Fr |
| Salt, coarse and all fine salt in bulk, other than above ...... 8 cts. per 100 lbs. | |
| Salt, in bags, barrels and other packages...12 cts. per 100 lbs. | |
| Salt Bags, containing fine salt .......................... | 25 |
| Saltpetre, nitrate of..................................... | 20 |
| Sand ..................................................... | Fr |
| Sand, colored............................................ | 20 |
| Sand Cloth............................................... | 25 |
| Sand (iron) or globules for polishing granite............. | Fr |
| Sandpaper, glass and Emery paper........................ | 25 |
| Sandalwood, sawn, not shaped, planed or otherwise manufactured................................................ | Fr |
| Sapolio .................................................. | 20 |
| Sarsparilla, Root ........................................ | Fr |
| Satin, Silk .............................................. | 30 |
| Satin, and fine-washed white (colors).................... | Fr |
| Satin-wood, sawn, not shaped, planed or otherwise manufactured................................................ | Fr |
| Satteens, colored as Jeans ..............2 cts. per sq. yd. and | 15 |
| Satchels, Trunks, Valises and Carpet Bags................ | 30 |
| Sausage Casings.......................................... | 20 |
| Saw Dust, as manufactures of wood....................... | 25 |
| Saws of all kinds........................................ | 30 |
| Scales, balances, Weighing Beams and Steelyards........... | 30 |
| Scheidam Schnapps ................ ...........$1.90 per I,G. | |
| School Slates ............................................ | 25 |
| Scrap Iron.............................$1.00 per ton. | |
| Scrap Brass ............................................. | Fr |
| Screens, Japan .......................................... | 35 |
| Screws, steel and iron, called wood screws............... | 35 |
| Screws, Machine, intended for holding in wood, without nuts or other iron fixtures, to be classed as wood-screws | 35 |
| The same imported with nuts are properly screw bolts... | 30 |
| Screws, with Nuts....................................... | 30 |
| Scythes, steel, of all kinds............................. | 30 |
| Sea Grass................................................ | Fr |
| Seal Oil, produce of the fisheries of U. S................ | Fr |
| Seal Oil, from Newfoundland ........................... | Fr |
| Sealskins, fur, wholly or partially dressed............... | 15 |
| Sealskin, imitation in wool .............7½ cts. per lb. and | 20 |
| Seamless Drawn Tubing, brass........................... | 10 |

P.C.

Seamless Drawn Tubing, copper......................... 10
Seamless Drawn Tubing, zinc........................... 10
Seamless Cotton Bags..................2 cts. per lb. and 15
Seeds, flower, garden, field and other seeds for agricultural
    purposes when in bulk or other large parcels.......... 15
Seeds, the same, in small papers and parcels.............. 25
Seeds, mustard, unground.............................. 15
Seeds, mustard, ground................................ 25
Seeds for agricultural purposes do not include Anise, Carda-
    mon, Colchicum, Cummin, Fenugreek, Hyoscyamus,
    Philandri, Stramonium, Worm, Carraway. Canary.
Seeds, Canary and Carraway........................... 20
Seeds, other......................................... 20
Sea-weed, moss, and all other vegetable substances used for
    beds and mattresses, in their natural state or only
    cleaned ........................................... Free
Semaphore Wire...................................... 25
Senna, in leaves..................................... Free
Sesame, Seed Oil..................................... 20
Settlers' Effects—Wearing Apparel, Household Furniture,
    except Sewing Machines and Pianos, Professional
    Books, Implements and Tools of Trade, occupation
    or employment, which the settler has had in actual use
    for at least six months before removing to Canada;
    not to include machinery or live stock, or articles im-
    ported for use in any manufactory, establishment, or for
    sale; provided that any dutiable article entered as Set-
    tlers' Effects shall not be sold or otherwise dis-
    posed of without payment of duty until after two years
    actual use in Canada. Provided that under regulations
    to be made by the Minister of Customs, live stock, when
    imported in Manitoba or the North West Territory by
    intending settlers shall be free, until otherwise ordered
    by the Governor in Council ......................... Free
Sewer Pipes, glazed or unglazed ...................... 20
Sewing Machines, whole, or heads or parts of heads of Sew-
    ing Machines .........................$2 each and 20
Sewing Machines, parts of, viz.:—Stands and table tops, im-
    ported separately : stands to be treated as castings, and
    woodwork as manufactures of wood, both ............ 25
Sewing Thread on spools......-....................... 20
Sewing. Cotton Thread in hanks, black and bleached, three
    and six cord...................................... 12½
Shades, Glass, for lamps and gas lights ................ 30
Shawls, Cashmere and Paisley, if not composed chiefly of
    silk ............................................. 25
Shawls, Indian or Parametta.......................... 25

P.C.

| | |
|---|---|
| Shawls, Silk............................................ | 30 |
| Shawls, Woolen ....................................... | 25 |
| Shawls, knitted......................7½ cts. per lb. and | 20 |
| Shawls, other.......................................... | 25 |
| Sheep ................................................. | 20 |
| Sheep, for improvement of stock ..................... | Fre |
| Sheep Skins, tanned or dressed but not waxed or glazed.... | 15 |
| Sheep Skins, dressed and waxed or glazed.................. | 20 |
| Sheetings, Cotton, bleached and unbleached, not stained, painted or printed ...................1 ct. per sq. yd. and | 15 |
| Shellac Varnish.........................$1.90 per I.G. | |
| Shells, manufactured ................................. | 20 |
| Shingles............................................... | 20 |
| Sheet Music ........................................6 cts. per lb. | |
| Sheet Iron, No. 17 guage and thinner...................... | 12½ |
| Sheet Iron, thicker than 17 guage ..................... | 17½ |
| Ships and all other vessels, built in a foreign country, whether steam or sailing vessels, on application for Canadian register, on the fair market value of the hull and all appurtenances except machinery ................... | 10 |
| Machinery on same................................ | 25 |
| Ships, repairs on (according to material). | |
| Shirts, cotton, woven or made on frames.................. | 30 |
| Shirts, Drawers and Hosiery, wool, wholly or in part.......... 7½ cts. per lb. and | 20 |
| Shirt Fronts, Collars and Cuffs, paper, linen or cotton...... | 30 |
| Shirtings, cotton, checked and striped...2 cts. per sq. yd. and | 15 |
| Shoddy................................................ | 20 |
| Shoes and Boots, leather and rubber.................... | 25 |
| Shoes, Felt............................................ | 25 |
| Shoemakers' Ink....................................... | 25 |
| Shoemakers' Pitch .................................... | 20 |
| Shoe Linings, twilled cotton.............1 ct. per sq. yd. and | 15 |
| Shoe Linings, colored jeanettes..........2 cts. per sq. yd. and | 15 |
| Shot, Lead............................................ | 30 |
| Shot Guns, not elsewhere specified .................... | 20 |
| Shot Pouches, leather................................. | 25 |
| Show Cases of any material ........................... | 35 |
| Show Cards or Bills (pictorial)...........6 cts. per lb. and | 20 |
| Show Cards, framed................................... | 35 |
| Shovels and Spades (steel)....., ...................... | 30 |
| Shoulders and Sides, fresh, salted, dried or smoked......... 2 cts. per lb. | |
| Shrubs and Trees, ornamental and shade, not elsewhere specified.................................................. | 20 |
| Silex or Crystallized Quartz........................... | Fre |
| Silicate of Soda ...................................... | Fre |

P.C.

Silicias and Casbans, plain, beetled or printed ........... 20
Silk, Lace ................................................ 20
Silk, raw, or as reeled from the cocoon, not being doubled, twisted or advanced in manufacture in any way, silk cocoons and silk waste ............................. Free
Silk Twist and Sewing Silk ........................... 25
Silk, Tram Silk, colored ............................. 25
Silk Umbrellas and Parasols .......................... 25
Silk Velvets, and all manufactures of silk, of which silk is the component part of chief value, not elsewhere specified ................................................ 30
Silk, in the gum, not more advanced than singles, tram, and thrown organzine, and raw spun silk not colored ....... 15
Silk—Manufactures of, embrace glacé, gros grain, ducape, barathea, Cachmere, Gros de Naples, black and coloured ; black and coloured Turquoise, satins, sarsenets, Persians, poplins, and all other piece goods of which silk is the component part of chief value ; all silk clothing, velvets, terries, chenilles, ribbons, silk plush, hat bands, velvet ribbons, tassels, shawls, hosiery and underclothing, ties, scarfs, bows, ferrets, handkerchiefs, Prussian bindings, sofa gimp, mantillas or jackets, silk warp Paramatta, silk tapestry, silk warp alpaca, &c. 30
Silk, plush netting, used for the manufacture of gloves ....... 15
Silver Coin (United States) ............................ 20
Silver and Gold Coins, except United States silver coin .... Free
Silver Leaf, for painters and gilders ................... 25
Silver-plated Ware ................................... 30
Silver Plate Glass ...... .......................... 30
Silver, rolled, and German Silver in sheets ............. 10
Silver Soap ........................................... 20
Skates of all kinds .................................. 30
Skins, undressed, dried, salted or pickled ............. Free
Skins, Fur Skins, wholly or partially dressed .......... 15
Slates, for roofing, black or blue ............ 80 cts. per sq.
Slates, for roofing green and other colors ....... $1 per sq.
Slates, school, and porcelain and drawing slates .......... 25
Slate Mantels ........................................ 30
Slate Slabs, square or in special shapes ............... 25
Slates of all kinds and manufactures of, N.E.S .......... 25
Sleighs .............................................. 30
Smalts, dry color .................................... 20
Snuff and manufactured tobaccos ......... 25 cts. per lb. and 12½
Soap, common brown and yellow, not perfumed ...........
                                          1½ cts. per lb.
Soap, common soft and liquid, not perfumed ............ 20
Soap, Castile and White ................. 2 cts. per lb.

|                                                                                  | P.C. |
|----------------------------------------------------------------------------------|------|
| Soap, perfumed or toilet                                                         | 30   |
| Soap, Powder                                                                     | 20   |
| Soda Ash                                                                         | Free |
| Soda, Bicarbonate of                                                             | 20   |
| Soda, Caustic                                                                    | Free |
| Soda, Nitrate of                                                                 | Free |
| Soda, Silicate of                                                                | Free |
| Soil Pipes, cast iron                                                            | 25   |
| Sole Leather, tanned but rough and undressed                                     | 10   |
| Sole Leather, tanned but not waxed or glazed                                     | 15   |
| Sole Leather tanned, waxed and glazed                                            | 20   |
| Soups                                                                            | 20   |
| Spades and Shovels (steel)                                                       | 30   |
| Spanish Cedar, not shaped, planed or otherwise manufac-tured                     | Free |
| Spanish or Esparto Grass, and other grasses and pulp of, for the manufacture of paper | Free |
| Spar and Alabaster Ornaments                                                     | 20   |
| Spectacles and Eye Glasses                                                       | 20   |
| Spelter, in blocks or pig                                                        | Free |
| Spermaceti                                                                       | 20   |
| Sperm Oil                                                                        | 20   |
| Spices of all kinds, except Mace and Nutmegs, unground                           | 20   |
| Spices, as above, ground                                                         | 25   |
| Spices, Mace and Nutmegs                                                         | 25   |
| Spikes and Nails, cut ...½ ct. per lb. and                                       | 10   |
| Spikes and Nails, wrought or pressed, whether galvanized or not ...¾ ct. per lb. and | 10   |
| Spikes and Nails, composition and sheathing                                      | 20   |
| Spikes, for original construction of Canadian Pacific R.R.                       | Free |

Spirits and Strong Waters, not having been sweetened or
    mixed with any article so that the degree of strength
    thereof cannot be ascertained by Sykes' Hydrometer, for
    every Imperial Gallon of the strength of proof by such
    Hydrometer, and so in proportion for any greater or less
    strength than a gallon, viz.: Geneva Gin, Rum, Whis-
    key and unenumerated articles of like kinds.............
                      $1.32½ per I.G.

Spirits, Brandy.............................$1.45 per I.G.
Spirits, whiskey, Geneva Gin and Rum ...$1.32 1/2 per I.G.
Spirits, Old Tom Gin...................$1.32 1/2 per I.G.
Spirits, sweetened or mixed so that the degree of strength
    cannot be ascertained as aforesaid, viz.  Rum-shrub,
    Cordials Scheidam Schnapps, Tafia, Bitters, and unen-
    umerated articles of like kind.........$1.90 per I.G.
Spirits, Strong Waters imported into Canada mixed with any
    ingredient, or ingredients, and although thereby coming

P.C.

under the denomination of Proprietary Medicines, Tinctures, Essences, Extracts, or any other denomination, Medicinal Elixirs and Fluid Extracts and Wine preparations, in bulk or bottle, not elsewhere specified shall be nevertheless deemed spirits or strong waters and subject to same duty as such............$1.90 per I.G. and 20

Spirits and Strong Waters, not elsewhere specified..........
$1.90 per I.G.

Spirits of Turpentine ....................................... 20
Sponges ..................................................... 20
Spokes, Hubs, Felloes, rough or sawn only............... 15
Spokes, Felloes, Hubs, finished......................... 25
Sprigs, Tacks and Brads .............................. 30
Stained Glass.......................................... 30
Starch, Corn Starch and all preparations having the quality of starch.............................2 cts. per lb.

Stationery of all kinds, not elsewhere specified............. 20
The following articles, not specially named in the tariff, may be classed as stationery, viz:—Penholders and pencil cases of all kinds, paper binders and fasteners (metal), pencil sharpeners, mucilage, paper weights and slips, copying pencils, inkstands (except electroplated), notarial seals, philosophical and mathematical instruments, drawing pens, tape measures, ink powder, parchment, chalks and crayons, India and China ink, quills and quill and steel pens, ivory knives and folders, wafers and stamps, slate pencils, juvenile and all water colors for artists, pink tape, pastilles, globes, rulers, pen-trays, key rings and chains...................

Steel, in ingots, bars, sheets, coils, Rails and Fish Plates, shall be free of duty until the close of the session of Parliament next ensuing, unless sooner repealed.

Steel or Bessemer Steel Locomotive Tires, in the rough .... 10
Steel Castings......................................... 25
Steel, all manufactures of, not elsewhere specified........... 20
Steel and Iron, (combined) all manufactures of, not elsewhere specified.................................... 20
Steel Wire, galvanized or not ....................... 15
Steel Plates, manufactured ........................... 20
Steel in coils, such as imported for the manufacture of screws and rake teeth, if cut to special length, or bent to shape, is dutiable as manufacture of steel..................... 20
Steel Mould Boards, Land Slides and Shares for Ploughs, cut to form, not moulded or bored.................... Free
Steel Sheets, of all kinds, cut to shape, but not moulded or bored "as they come from the roller and shears," free as sheet steel. This includes saw blanks............. Free

P.C.

Steelyards, to be included in the item "scales, balances and weighing beams " .................................... 30

Sereotypes and Electrotypes of Standard books, except those of Advertising books, almanacs and sheets............. 10

Stereotypes and Electrotypes for Commercial Blanks and Advertisements ................................. 20

Stick extract or confection, Liquorice......1 ct. per lb. and 20

Stone, Burr, in blocks, rough or unmanufactured, and not bound into millstone............................... Free

Stone, rough, Freestone, Sandstone, and all other building stone except Marble from the quarry not hammered or chiselled (13 cubic feet to ton).............$1 per ton.

Stone-ware and Rockingham Ware .................... 25

Stone, Waterlime or Cement Stone............$1.00 per ton.

Stone, dressed Freestone and all other building stone except Marble, and all manufactures of stone or granite.......... 20

Stone, Lithographic, not engraved......................... 20

Stone, Flagstones, dressed ... .............$1.50 per ton.

Stone, Grindstones......................$2.00 per ton.

Stoves and other castings and forgings, not elsewhere specified............................................... 25

Straw and manufactures of, not elsewhere specified.......... 20

Straw Hats.................................... 25

Strawberries, green fruit ....................2 cts. per qt.

Straw Board, not Mill board.......................... 20

Studs, Shirt or Collar, of all kinds...................... 20

Sugar, above No. 14 Dutch Standard in color.............
  1 ct. per lb. and 35
  Including Export duty or other Government tax.

Sugar, equal to No. 9, not above No. 14 Dutch Standard ...
  ¾ ct. per lb. and 30
  Including Export duty or other Government tax.

Sugar, below No. 9 Dutch Standard......1/2 ct. per lb. and 30
  Including Export duty or other Government tax.

  Provided that the *ad valorem* duty shall be levied and collected on Sugar and Melado, when imported direct from the country of growth and production, upon the fair market value thereof at the place of purchase, without any addition for the cost of hogsheads or other packages, or other charges and expenses prior to shipment, anything contained in Sect. 34 of Act 40 Vic., Cap. 10, to the contrary notwithstanding, the said section nevertheless remaining in force as to regulations to be made under it in cases where the Sugar or Melado is not imported direct from the country of growth or production.

P.C.

Sugar Candy, brown or white, and Confectionery..........
                                1 ct. per lb. and  35
Sugar, Glucose, or Grape sugar to be classed and rated for duty
    as Sugar, according to grade by Dutch Standard in color.
Sulphate of Quinine (in powder).............................  Free
Sulphuric Acid .............................½ ct. per lb.
Sulphur, in roll or flour ....................................  Free
Sumac, Extract of...........................................  20
Sumac, tanning article in a crude state.....................  Free
Sunday School Cards or Devotional Cards.—No exception
    can be made from the item "printed, lithographed, etc.
    cards." ...................................................  30
Superphosphates, or manufactured Manure....................  20
Surgical Instruments and Dental Instruments, wholly or in
    part of steel ............................................  20
Sweet Potatoes .............................................  20
Swine......................................................  20
Swine, for improvement of stock ............................  Free
Syrups, Cane Juice, Refined Syrup, Sugar-house Syrup, Syrup
    of Sugar, Syrup of Molasses and Sorghum ...............
                            ⅜ ct. per lb. and  30
    Melado, Concentrated Melado, Concentrated Cane Juice,
      Concentrated Molasses, Concentrated Beet-root Juice,
      and Concrete ....................⅜ ct. per lb. and  30
    Molasses, if used for refining, clarifying or rectifying
      purposes or for the manufacture of sugar, when im-
      ported direct from the country of growth or produc-
      tion.....................................................  25
      Including Export duty or other Government tax.
Molasses, for same purposes, when not imported direct
    rom country of growth or production..................  30
    Including Export dutp or other Government tax.
    Molasses, when not so used, when imported direct from
      country of growth or production ...................  15
      Including Export duty or other Government tax.
Molasses, when not so used, and when not imported direct
    from country of growth and production................  20
    Including Export duty or other Government tax.

# T

Tables, furniture .........................................  35
Table Tops and Stands, for sewing machine, imported sepa-
    rately.................................................  25
Tacks, Brads and Sprigs....................................  30
Tafia (see spirits)....................$ 1.90 per I.G.
Tails, undressed...........................................  Free

P.C.

| | |
|---|---|
| Tails Dressed, (see furs) | 15 |
| Tallow | 1 ct. per lb. |
| Tampico, white and black | Free |
| Tanner's Bark | Free |
| Tanning and Dyeing Articles in a crude state used in dyeing or tanning, not elsewhere specified | Free |
| Tanning or Dyeing Articles, prepared, not elsewhere specified | 20 |
| Tapers, Wax | 20 |
| Tape Measures, as Stationery | 20 |
| Tapioca | 20 |
| Taraxicum Root | Free |
| Tar and Pitch Pine | Free |
| Tar and Pitch Coal | 10 |
| Tarpaulin, Cotton, plain or coated with oil, paint, tar or other composition | 30 |
| Tassels, gold and silver | 20 |
| Tassels, silk | 30 |
| Tea, Green, Japan and Black, imported from other countries than the United States | Free |
| Tea, Green, Japan and Black, imported from United States. | 10 |
| Teasels | Free |
| Telephones | 25 |
| Telegraphic Instruments | 25 |
| Telegraph Apparatus for original construction of Canadian Pacific Railway | Free |
| Tents and Awnings | 25 |
| Terra Japonica | Free |
| Thimbles of all kinds | 20 |
| Thread, Cotton, sewing, on spools | 20 |
| Thread, Cotton, sewing, in hanks, black and bleached, three and six cords | 12½ |
| Thread, Linen | 20 |
| Thread, Gold and Silver Thread | 20 |
| Threshing Machines | 25 |
| Ticking, for tents | 2 cts. per sq. yd. and 15 |
| Tiles, Roofing | 20 |
| Tiles, other | 20 |
| Timber and Lumber, planks and boards, sawn, not shapen, planed or otherwise manufactured : African Teak, Black Heart Ebony, Boxwood, Cherry, Chestnut and Hickory, Lignumvitæ, Mahogany, Oak, Pitch Pine, Red Cedar, Rosewood, Satinwood, Sandalwood, Spanish Cedar, Walnut and Whitewood | Free |
| Timber and Lumber, not elsewhere specified | 20 |
| Tin, in blocks, pigs, bars and sheets | Free |

P.C.

In Cans or packages made of tin or other material, containing fish of any kind, admitted free under existing treaties,
not exceeding 1 quart in contents ...................1½ cts.
And if exceeding 1 quart, 1½ cts. additional for each qt.
or parts of :

Tin-foil........................................................................ Free

Tin-foil, Capsules ........................................... 25

Tinman's Trimmings, to be classed as manufactures of Tin,
viz :—Spouts, handles, knobs and ornamental articles... 25

Tinware, and all other manufactures of tin, not elsewhere
specified .................................................... 25

Tin Plates................................................... Free

Tobacco, Cigars and Cigarettes .............60 cts. per lb. and 20

Tobacco, Snuff...........................25 cts. per lb. and 12½

Tobacco, manufactured, other .....25 cts. per lb. and 12½

Tobacco, unmanufactured, for excise purposes. under conditions of Act 31, Vic. Cap. 51 ...................... Free

Tobacco Pipes, all kinds................................ 20

Toilet Powders (as perfumery) ......................... 30

Tomatoes...........................30 cts. per bush.

Tomatoes in cans .....................2 cts. per lb.

Tools, Bookbinders' tools and implements, including Ruling
Machines............................................. 10

Tools, carpenters', coopers', Cabinet Makers' and all other
mechanics' tools, including files, edge tools of every
description............................................ 30

Tooth Powders, as perfumery ........................... 30

Tortoise and other Shells, unmanufactured .............. Free

Tragacanth Gum........................................ Free

Tram silk, colored .................................... 25

Travellers' Baggage, under regulations to be prescribed by
the Minister of Customs............................. Free

Trees, Forest, for planting, imported into Manitoba or
North-West Territory................................ Free

Trees, Apple..............................2 cts. each.

Trees, Pear and Cherry....................4 cts. each.

Trees, Apple and Quince..................2½ cts. each.

Trees, Plum.............................5 cts. each.

Trees and Plants, other than above, including fruit, shade,
lawn and ornamental................................. 20

Treenails ............................................ Free

Tripoli............................................... 20

Trunks, Satchels, Valises and Carpet Bags.............. 30

Tubs, wood ........................................... 25

Tubing, seamless drawn tubing of copper, brass and zinc..... 10

Tubing, lap-welded boiler iron tubing, not threaded, coupled
or otherwise manufactured........................... 15

P.C.

Tubing, Iron, wrought iron tubing, not threaded, coupled or otherwise manufactured, plain, 2 inches in diameter or over .................................................... 15
Tubing, wrought iron tubing, plain, 2 in. or under in diameter, coupled and threaded or not........................... 25
Tubing, Iron, other, not elsewhere specified ............... 20
Turmeric...................................................... Free
Turpentine, raw or crude ..................................... Free
Turpentine, Spirits of......................................... 20
Turtles ...................................................... Free
Tweeds, wool .......................7½ cents per lb. and 20
Twines, Sail, when to be used for boats' and ships' sails.... 5
Twines, for use of fisheries................................. Free
Twines, all other............................................ 25
Type, for printing .......................................... 20
Type Metal .................................................. 10

## U

Ultramarine Blue, color in pulp ............................ Free
Umbrellas and Parasols of all kinds ........................ 25
Union Collar Cloth Paper, in sheets, not shapen ........... 10
Undertakers' Hardware, plated.............................. 30
Umber, raw, dry color....................................... Free
Upholsterers' Hardware...................................... 30

## V

Vaccine and Ivory Vaccine Points .......................... Free
Valerian Root .............................................. Free
Valentines and Christmas Cards............................. 25
Valises..................................................... 30
Vanilla and Nux Vomica Beans.............................. Free
Varnish, black and bright, for ships' use................... Free
Varnish, Lackers, Japan and Collodion, not elsewhere specified.........................20 cts. per I.G. and 20
Vasseline.................................................... 20
Vegetables, Potatoes, not elsewhere specified .............
    10 cts. per bush.
Vegetables, Oil, not elsewhere specified.................... 20
Vegetables, Onions.......................................... 20
Vegetables, prepared or preserved, not elsewhere specified].. 20
Vegetables, Split Peas ..................................... 20
Vegetables, Sweet Potatoes and all other Vegetables, not elsewhere specified ...................................... 20
Vegetables, Tomatoes .......................30 cts. per bush.
Vegetables, Tomatoes, in cans ................2 cts. per lb.

P.C.

Vegetable fibres, natural, not produced by any chemical pro-
cess............................................... Free
Velvets, silk........................................... 30
Velvets, cotton........................................ 20
Velveteens............................................ 20
Veneers of wood and ivory, sawn or split only, not to include
scale board for cheese............................. Free
Verdegris or sub-acetate of Copper ................. Free
Vermicelli and Macaroni ............................ 20
Vines, Grape Vines of all kinds..................... 20
Vinegar...................................12 cts. per I.G.
Vices................................................ 30
Vitriol, blue.......................................... Free
Volatile, or Essential Oil, for manufacturing purposes ......... 20

# W

Wadding, Cotton, unbleached, not dyed or colored .........
2 cts. per lb. and  15
Wagons ............................................. 30
Wall Paper.......................................... 30
Walking Sticks...................................... 25
Walnuts............................................. 20
Walnut Lumber, plank and board, sawn, not shaped.. .... Free
Warps, Cotton, not bleached, dyed or colored ............
2 cts. per lb. and  15
Warps, Cotton, if bleached, dyed or colored...3 c. p. lb. and  15
Washers, Bolts and Rivets............................ 30
Waste cotton, linen, jute, hemp and paper of all kinds, fit
only for the manufacture of paper.................... Free
Watches............................................. 25
Watch Cases......................................... 25
Watches, Chronometer................................ 25
Watch material and movements ...................... 20
Water, Mineral and Aërated.......................... 20
Water, Rose Water, as Perfumery..................... 30
Whale Bone, unmanufactured ........................ Free
Whale Bone, manufactured ........................... 20
Whale Oil, in casks, from on shipboard and in the condition
in which it was first landed ......................... Free
Whale Oil and Fish Oil from Newfoundland.............. Free
Whale Oil, other..................................... 20
Wax Candles ........................................ 25
Wax, Beeswax, and other, not elsewhere specified .......... 20
Wax, Paraffine Wax or Stearine.............3 cts. per lb.
Wax Tapers......................................... 20
Wax, manufactures of, other.......................... 20

P.C.

Wheat .................................................15 cts. per bush.

Wheat, damaged by water in transitu (on appraised value)....  20

Wheat Flour ...............................................50 cts. per bbl.

Wheat Flour, damaged by water in transitu (on appraised
    value) ...................................................  20

Wheels, parts of, Hubs and Spokes, in the rough ...........  15
    If smoothed and finished ..............................  25

Wheels if put up as part of carriage ......................  30

Wheels, Car, iron .........................................  25

Wheelbarrows, and other like articles .....................  30

Whips .....................................................  25

Whip Gut or Cat Gut, unmanufactured .......................  Free

Whiskey .............................................$1.32½ per I.G.

White Lead, in pulp, not mixed with oil ...................  5

White Lead and Red Lead, and orange mineral, dry .......  5

White Granite or Iron Stone Ware ..........................  30

Whitewood Lumber, plank and sawn, not shaped ..........  Free

Willow, for basket makers .................................  Free

Willow and Osier Furniture ................................  35

Willow and Osier Works, lined or unlined, furnished or un-
    furnished, not elsewhere specified .....................  25

Window Shades, made of paper ..............................  30

Winceys, plain, of all widths, when material is not over ¼ of
    wool ..................................................  20

Winceys, checked, striped or fancy, not over twenty-five (25)
    inches wide ...........................................  20

Winceys, checked, striped or fancy dress winceys, over
    twenty-five (25) inches wide and not over thirty (30) inch-
    es, when material is not more than ¼ wool ..........

                      2 cts. per sq. yd. and  15

Winceys, checked, striped or fancy winceys, over thirty (30)
    inches wide, when material is more than ¼ wool ......

                      7½ cts. per lb, and  20

Wines of all kinds, except sparkling wines, including ginger,
    orange, lemon, strawberry, raspberry, elder and currant,
    containing 26% or less of spirits of strength of proof by
    Sykes' Hydrometer, imported in wood or bottles (6 qts.
    or 12 pints to I.G.) ..................25 cts. per I.G. and  30

Wines, containing over 26 p.c. and not over 27 p.c .............
                      28 cts. per I.G. and  30

Wines, containing over 27 p.c. and not over 28 p.c ........
                      31 cts. per I.G. and  30

Wines, containing over 28 p.c. and not over 29 p.c ........
                      34 cts. per I.G. and  30

Wines, containing over 29 p.c. and not over 30 p.c ..........
                      37 cts. per I.G. and  30

P.C.

Wines, containing over 30 p.c. and not over 31 p.c ..........
40 cts. per I.G. and 30

Wines, containing over 31 p.c. and not over 32 p.c ..........
43 cts. per I.G. and 30

Wines, containing over 32 p.c. and not over 33 p.c ..........
46 cts. per I.G. and 30

Wines, containing over 33 p.c. and not over 34 p.c .........
49 cts. per I.G. and 30

Wines, containing over 34 p.c. and not over 35 p.c ..........
52 cts. per I.G. and 30

Wines, containing over 35 p.c. and not over 36 p.c .........
55 cts. per I.G. and 30

Wines, containing over 36 p.c. and not over 37 p.c .........
58 cts. per I.G. and 30

Wines, containing over 37 p.c. and not over 38 p.c ..........
61 cts. per I.G. and 30

Wines, containing over 38 p.c. and not over 39 p.c ..........
64 cts. per I.G. and 30

Wines, containing over 39 p.c. and not over 40 p.c ........
67 cts. per I.G. and 30

Champagne and all other sparkling wines, in bottles, containing each not more than 1 quart and more than 1 pint, old wine measure ........ $3.00 per doz. and 30

In bottes, containing not more than a pint and more than one-half pint, wine measure....... $1.50 per doz. and 30

In bottles, containing one-half pint each or less............
75 cts. per doz. and 30

In bottles, containing more than one quart................
$3 per doz., $1.50 per I.G. and 30

Note.—All Liquors imported under the name of Wine and containing more than 40 per cent. of spirit of strength of proof by Sykes' Hydrometer, shall be rated as unenumerated spirits.

Wire Cloth of brass or copper ............................ 20
Wire, Iron and Steel, tinned, coppered, galvanized or not... 15
Wire, for telegraph line, first equipment Canadian Pacific Railway.............................................. Free
Wire, round or flat, of brass or copper...................... 10
Wire, Brass, and rods cut to special length .................. 30
Wire Rods, iron in coils, under half an inch in diameter....... 10
Wire Rigging for ships and vessels.......................... Free
Wire Rope, strand or chain made of wire.................... 25
Wire, manufactures of, other, not elsewhere specified........ 25
Wood, for fuel, when imported into Manitoba and North-West Territory........................................ Free
Wood, Cord Wood, other ................................. 20
Wood manufactures, viz.: Fishing Rods.................... 30

P.C.

Wood Furniture, house, cabinet or office, ncluding hair, spring and other mattresses, show cases, bolsters and pillows, caskets and coffins, of any material, and picture frames ............................................................. 35

Wood, Hubs, Spokes, Felloes and parts of Wheels, rough hewn or sawn only ............................... 15

Wood, Shingles ......................................... 20

Wood, Pails, Tubs and Churns ......................... 25

Wood, manufactures of, not elsewhere specified ........... 25

Wood, Lumber and Timber, not eisewhere specified ....... 20

Wood, Lumber and Timber, planks and boards sawn, of Box-wood, Cherry, Walnut, Chestnut, Mahogany, Pitch Pine, Rosewood, Sandalwood, Spanish Cedar, Oak, Hickory, Whitewood, African Teak, Black Heart Ebony, Lig-numvitæ, Red Cedar and Satinwood ................... Free

Wood, Lumber and Timber, not elsewhere specified, to in-clude lumber and timber of the kinds otherwise free, when cut to special lengths—*i.e.*, less than the ordinary commercial lengths .............................. 20

Wood, Logs and round unmanufactured timber, not else-where mentioned .................................... Free

Wool, unmanufactured, hair of Alpaca Goat and other like animals, not elsewhere specified ..................... Free

Wool and Woolens, composed wholly or in part of Wool, Worsted, hair of Alpaca Goat or other like animals, viz.: Cloths, Doeskins, Blankets, and Flannels of every des-cription, Doeskins, Cassimeres, Tweeds, Coatings, Overcoatings, Cloakings, Felt Cloths of every descrip-tion, not elsewhere specified, Horse Collar Cloths, Yarn, Knitting Yarn, Fingering Yarn, Worsted Yarn, under No. 30 ........................7½ cts. per lb. and   20

Wool and Woolens—Clothing ready-made, Wearing Apparel of every description, including Cloth Caps and Horse Clothing shaped, composed wholly or in part of wool, worsted, hair of Alpaca goat or other like animals, made up or manufactured wholly or in part by the tailor, seamstress, or the manufacturer, except knitted goods... 10 cts. per lb. and *ad valorem*   25

Wool and Woolens—All manufactures of, composed wholly or in part of wool, worsted, hair of Alpaca goat, or oth-er like animals, not otherwise provided for ........... 20

Wool Manufactures not otherwise provided for:—Orleans, Alpacas, Lustres, Cobourgs, Baratheas, Balmoral Crapes, Persian Cords, Russell Cords, Twills, Moreens, Para-mattas (not silk warp), Henriettas, Figured Alpacas, Debaiges, Muslin Delaines, French Delaines and French Merinoes, Cashmeres, Cloth Table Covers and Piano

| P.C. | | P.C. |
|---|---|---|
| | Covers, Victoria Table Covers, Bullion Fringe, Fancy Wool Fringe, Mohair Braid, Llama Braid, Russian Braid, unless the largest component part be silk, Bunting, and all kinds of Bradford Dress Goods . . . . . . . . . . | 20 |
| 35 | | |
| 15 | Wool, Class one, viz., Leicester, Cotswold, Lincolnshire, Down Combing Wools, and other like combing wools such as are grown in Canada . . . . . . . . . . . . . 3 cts. per lb. | |
| 20 | | |
| 25 | Woolen Hosiery, held to comprise men's, women's and children's Lambs-wool, Cashmere and Merino Shirts and Drawers, Wool Scarfs, Mufflers, Cravats, Clouds, Handkerchiefs, Collarettes, Cardigan Jackets, Polkas, Knitted Shawls, Vests, 'Cross-overs," Chest Protectors, Knitted Mantles, Petticoats, Cuffs, Boots and Bootees . . . . . . . . . | |
| 25 | | |
| 20 | | |
| | 7½ cts. per lb. and | 20 |
| Free | Woolen Rags . . . . . . . . . . . . . . . . . . . . . . . . . . . . . . . . . . . . . . | Free |
| | Woolen Shawls, except knitted . . . . . . . . . . . . . . . . . . . . . . . . | 25 |
| | Woolen Carpets, Brussels and Tapestry . . . . . . . . . . . . . . . . | 20 |
| 20 | Woolen Carpets, two-ply and three-ply, treble ingrain, composed wholly of wool . . . . . . . . . . 10 cts. per sq. yd. and | 20 |
| Free | Woolen Carpets, Ingrain, of which the warp is composed wholly of cotton or other material than wool worsted the hair of the Alpaca goat or other like animals . . . . . . . . . | |
| Free | 5 cts. per sq. yd. and | 20 |
| | Woolen Imitation Sealskins . . . . . . . . . . . . 7½ cts. per lb. and | 20 |
| | Woolen Felt, for boots, shoes and skirts, when imported by the manufacturers for use in their factories . . . . . . . . . . . | 15 |
| | Woolen Felt, for glove lining, and Endless Felt for paper makers, when imported by the manufacturers for use in their factories . . . . . . . . . . . . . . . . . . . . . . . . . – . . . . . . . . . . . . | 10 |
| 20 | Woolen Netting, for boots and shoes . . . . . . . . . . . . . . . . . . . . | 10 |
| | Worm Seed . . . . . . . . . . . . . . . . . . . . . . . . . . . . . . . . . . . . . . . . | 20 |
| | Worsted Plush . . . . . . . . . . . . . . . . . . . . . . . . . . . . . . . . . . . . . . | 20 |
| | Wrapping Paper . . . . . . . . . . . . . . . . . . . . . . . . . . . . . . . . . . . . | 20 |
| | Writing Ink . . . . . . . . . . . . . . . . . . . . . . . . . . . . . . . . . . . . . . . | 25 |
| | Writing Desks, to be rated according to material. | |
| | Wrought Iron, Forgings and parts of, for mills, and Locomotives—parts weighing 25 lbs. or more . . . . . . . . . . . . . | 20 |
| 25 | | |

## X

| 20 | Xyolite, or Celluloid in sheets . . . . . . . . . . . . . . . . . . . . . . . . | Free |

## Y

| | Yarns, Knitting, Cotton, Hosiery Yarn, or other cotton yarn under No. 40, not bleached, dyed or colored . . . . . . | |
| | 2 cts. per lb. and | 15 |

E

|  | P.C. |
|---|---|
| Yarns, Knitting Yarn, Hosiery Yarn, bleached, dyed or colored..................................3 cts. per lb. and | 15 |
| Yarn, Fingering Yarn, wool.............7½ c. per lb. and | 20 |
| Yarn, Knitting Yarn, wool.............7½ c. per lb. and | 20 |
| Yarn, Worsted Yarn, under No. 30......7½ c. per lb. and | 20 |
| Yarns, Coir ............................................. | Free |
| Yeast................................................... | 20 |
| Yellow Metal, n bolts, bars and for sheathing ............ | Free |

## Z

| | |
|---|---|
| Zinc, in blocks, pigs and sheets.......................... | Free |
| Zinc, seamless drawn tubing............................. | 10 |
| Zinc, dry white (color)................................. | 5 |
| Zinc, manufactures of, not elsewhere mentioned............. | 25 |
| Zinc Dust............................................... | 25 |

All goods not enumerated in this Act or any other Act as charged with any duty of Customs and not declared free of duty by this Act or some unrepealed Act or provision, shall be charged with a duty of twenty per cent. *ad valorem*, when imported into Canada, or taken out of warehouse for consumption therein.

———

*The following articles shall be prohibited to be imported under a penalty of two hundred dollars, together with the forfeiture of the parcel or package of goods in which the same may be found, viz.:*

Books, printed papers, drawings, paintings, prints, photographs or representations of any kind of a treasonable or seditious, or of an immoral or indecent character.

Coin, base or counterfeit.

*The following articles, being the natural products of the manufactures of the colony of Newfoundland, are exempted from Customs duty when imported into Canada, viz. :*

Fish, fresh, dried, salted or smoked.
Fish Oil and all products of Fish.
Seal Oil.
Animals of all kinds.

# EXCISE DUTIES. &c.

1. That any party in whose favor a license is granted to have and use a chemical still, shall, upon receiving the said license, pay to the Collector of Inland Revenue the sum of ten dollars.

2. That any party in whose favor a license for manufacturing Tobacco wholly or in part from foreign leaf is granted, shall pay therefor to the Collector of Internal Revenue the sum of seventy-five dollars.

3. That any party in whose favor a license for manufacturing Tobacco exclusively from Canadian leaf is granted, shall pay therefor to the Collector of Inland Revenue the sum of fifty dollars.

4. That any party in whose favor a license for manufacturing in bond for exportation is granted shall pay therefor to the Collector of Inland Revenue the sum of three hundred dollars.

5. That any party in whose favor a license to have an EXCISE BONDING WAREHOUSE is granted shall pay to the Collector of Inland Revenue for one such Warehouse the sum of forty dollars, and for each additional Warehouse the sum of twenty dollars.

6. That as respects the duties of EXCISE ON SPIRITS:

*(a.)* When the material used in the manufacture thereof consists of not less than ninety per cent. by weight of raw or unmalted grain, on every gallon of the strength of proof by Sykes' Hydrometer, and so in proportion for any greater or less strength than the strength of proof, and for every less quantity than a gallon, *one dollar.*

*(b.)* When manufactured exclusively from malted barley taken to the distillery in bond and on which no duty of Customs or Excise has been paid, on every gallon of the strength of proof by Sykes' Hydrometer, and so in proportion for any greater or less strength, and for any less quantity than a gallon, *one dollar and two cents.*

*(c.)* When manufactured exclusively from molasses or sugar taken to the distillery in bond, and on which no duty of Customs has been paid, on every gallon of the strength of proof by Sykes' Hydrometer, and so in proportion for any greater or less strength, and for any less quantity than a gallon, *one dollar and three cents.*

7. That as respects the duties of Excise on manufactured Tobacco, the said duties shall be as follows:

On manufactured TOBACCO AND SNUFF of all kinds, except Cigars, made in whole or part from foreign or imported leaf Tobacco and containing not less than ten per cent. by weight of moisture, and so in proportion for any greater or less degree of moisture, in every pound or less quantity than a pound, *twenty cents.*

ON CIGARS made in whole or in part from foreign or imported leaf Tobacco and containing not less than ten per cent. by weight of moisture, and so on in proportion for every greater or less degree of moisture, on every pound or less quantity than a pound, *forty cents.*

CIGARS made solely from Tobacco grown in Canada, *twenty cents per pound.*

"Tabac blanc en Torquette," or Canadian Twist, being the unstemmed, unflavored and unpressed leaf of tobacco grown in Canada, twisted and made into coils by the cultivator thereof, *four cents per pound.*

TOBACCO made exclusively from leaf grown in Canada during next two years to pay *eight cents per pound*, and after, *ten cents per pound.*

8.   That as respects the duties of EXCISE ON VINEGAR:

Vinegar containing six per cent. of acetic acid, the strength to be determined by such tests as may from time to time be established by Orders in Council, and so in proportion for any greater or less strength, on every gallon or less than a gallon, *four cents.*

9.   That as respects the duty of EXCISE ON METHYLATED SPIRITS:

Methylated Spirits being composed of alcohol mixed with wood naphtha in such proportions, and subject to such regulations, as may from time to time be made by the Department of Inland Revenue, there shall be paid a duty of *fifteen cents* for every gallon of the strength of proof, and so in proportion for every greater or less strength, and for every less quantity than a gallon.

10.   That any provisions imposing any new duty, or making any alteration in the mode of calculating any such duty by which the amount thereof may be increased or diminished, shall come into force immediately on the day of passing of the Act making such alterations, and shall apply to and the duties hereby imposed shall be payable on all Spirits and Tobacco, Vinegar, Fermented Beverages or Methylated Spirits, distilled, manufactured or made, or taken out of bond for consumption on and after the said day, and such alterations as aforesaid shall apply to and the duties hereby imposed shall be payable on all malt held by any brewer, maltster, distiller, or other person on the said day, or manufactured or made thereafter, and the duties hereby made payable on licenses shall be payable only on licenses issued after the said day, existing licenses remaining in force during the time for which they were granted.

All goods manufactured in bond shall, if taken out of bond for consumption in Canada, be subject to duties of Excise equal to the duties of Customs to which they would be subject if imported from Great Britan and entered for consumption in Canada; and whenever any article not the produce of Canada, upon which a duty of Excise would be levied if produced in Canada, is taken into a Bonded Manufactory, the difference between the duty of Excise to which it would be so liable and the Customs duty which would be levied on such articles if imported and entered for consumption, shall be paid as duty of Excise when it is taken into the Bonded Manufactory.

Distilling or Rectifying.................................... $250
Compounding ...........................................   50
For Importation or Manufacture of Apparatus...............   30
For Brewing................................................   50
For Malting, 1st Class ................................... 200
    "      "    2nd  "   ..............................  150
    "      "    3rd  "   ..............................  100
    "      "    4th  "   ..............................   50
For Manufacturing in Bond for Consumption in Canada......   50
    "          "          "    "    "  Exportation..............  300
On Fermented Beverage made in imitation of Beer or Malt
    Liquor.........................................8cts. per gal.

Inspection fee on Petroleum :

On every package containing not more than 5 gals...2½ cts.
On every package containing not more than 10 gals...5 cts.
On every package containing not more than 50 gals...10 cts.
And five cents extra for every 50 gallons...................

# LIST OF WAREHOUSING PORTS.

———•———

## PROVINCE OF QUEBEC.

Coaticooke,          Quebec,              Sherbrooke,
Gaspé,               Richmond,            Sorel,
Magdalen Islands,    Rimouski,            Stanstead,
Montreal,            Rouse's Point,       St. Johns,
New Carlisle,        St. Armand,          Three Rivers.
Percé,               St. Hyacinthe,

## PROVINCE OF ONTARIO.

Amherstburg,         Fort Erie,           Peterboro,
Barrie,              Galt,                Picton,
Belleville,          Gananoque,           Port Credit,
Berlin,              Goderich,            Port Hope,
Brampton,            Guelph,              Port Ryerse,
Brantford,           Hamilton,            Prescott,
Brockville,          Ingersoll,           Prince Arthur's L'dg,
Cardinal,            Kincardine,          Queenston,
Chatham,             Kingston,            Sarnia,
Clifton,             Leamington,          Sault Ste. Marie,
Clinton,             Lindsay,             Simcoe,
Cobourg,             London,              Stratford,
Colborne,            Midland,             St. Catherines,
  (Welland Canal.)   Morrisburg,          St. Marys,
Collingwood,         Napanee,             St. Thomas,
Cornwall,            Newcastle,           Toronto,
Cramahe,             Niagara,             Trenton,
  (Colborne Co.)     Oakville,            Walkerton,
Darlington,          Oshawa,              Wallaceburg,
Deseronto,           Ottawa,              Whitby,
Dover,               Owen Sound,          Windsor,
Dundas,              Paris,               Woodstock.
Dunville,            Pembroke,

### Province of New Brunswick.

| | | |
|---|---|---|
| Bathurst, | Grand Falls, | Shediac, |
| Buctouche, | Edmunston, | St. Andrews, |
| Campbellton, | Hillsborough. | St. George, |
| Campobello, | Moncton, | St. John, |
| Caraquette, | McAdams Junction. | St. Stephens, |
| Chatham, | Newcastle, | Sussex, |
| Dalhousie, | Richibucto, | Tracadie, |
| Dorchester, | Richmond Station, | Woodstock. |
| Fredericton, | Sackville, | |

### Province of Nova Scotia.

| | | |
|---|---|---|
| Advocate Harbour, | Kentville, | Port Hawkesbury. |
| Amherst, | Lahave, | Port Hastings, |
| Annapolis, | Liverpool, | Port Hood, |
| Antigonish | Londonderry, | Port Medway, |
| Arichat, | Locke Port, | Port William, |
| Bear River, | Lunenburg, | Pugwash, |
| Baddeck, | Mahone Bay, | Shelbourne, |
| Barrington, | Maitland, | St. Anns, |
| Bridgetown, | Margaretsville, | St. Peters, |
| Cornwallis, | New Glasgow, | Sydney, |
| Digby, | North Sydney, | Tatamagouche, |
| Economy. | Parsborough, | Truro, |
| Guysboro, | Pictou, | Wallace, |
| Great Bras d'Or, | Point Brulé, | Weymouth, |
| Halifax, | Port George, | Windsor, |
| Hastings, | Port Gilbert, | Yarmouth. |
| Ingonish Harbor, | | |

### British Columbia.

| | | |
|---|---|---|
| Burrards Inlet, | Stickeen, | Victoria. |
| New Westminster, | | |

### Prince Edward Island.

| | | |
|---|---|---|
| Charlottetown, | Georgetown, | Summerside. |

### Manitoba.

| | |
|---|---|
| Emerson, | Winnipeg. |

# TABLE

SHEWING THE

## VALUE IN DOLLARS AND CENTS

OF ALL

### Sums from One Penny to Fifty Thousand Pounds Stg.

CALCULATED

At 9½, or New Par of Exchange.

| £ | $ c. | £ | $ c. | £ | $ c. |
|---|------|---|------|---|------|
| 1... | 4.87 | 21... | 102.20 | 41... | 199.53 |
| 2... | 9.73 | 22... | 107.07 | 42... | 204.40 |
| 3... | 14.60 | 23... | 111.93 | 43... | 209.27 |
| 4... | 19.47 | 24... | 116.80 | 44... | 214.13 |
| 5... | 24.33 | 25... | 121.67 | 45... | 219.00 |
| 6... | 29.20 | 26... | 126.53 | 46... | 223.87 |
| 7... | 34.07 | 27... | 131.40 | 47... | 228.73 |
| 8... | 38.93 | 28... | 136.27 | 48... | 233.60 |
| 9... | 43.80 | 29... | 141.13 | 49... | 238.47 |
| 10... | 48.67 | 30... | 146.00 | 50... | 243.33 |
| 11... | 53.53 | 31... | 150.87 | 51... | 248.20 |
| 12... | 58.40 | 32... | 155.73 | 52... | 253.07 |
| 13... | 63.27 | 33... | 160.60 | 53... | 257.93 |
| 14... | 68.13 | 34... | 165.47 | 54... | 262.80 |
| 15... | 73.00 | 35... | 170.33 | 55... | 267.67 |
| 16... | 77.87 | 36... | 175.20 | 56... | 272.53 |
| 17... | 82.73 | 37... | 180.07 | 57... | 277.40 |
| 18... | 87.60 | 38... | 184.93 | 58... | 282.27 |
| 19... | 92.47 | 39... | 189.80 | 59... | 287.13 |
| 20... | 97.33 | 40... | 194.67 | 60... | 292.00 |

ENTS

)unds Stg.

GE.

| £ | $ c. |
|---|---|
|  | 199.53 |
|  | 204.40 |
|  | 209.27 |
|  | 214.13 |
|  | 219.00 |
|  | 223.87 |
|  | 228.73 |
|  | 233.60 |
|  | 238.47 |
|  | 243.33 |
|  | 248.20 |
|  | 253.07 |
|  | 257.93 |
|  | 262.80 |
|  | 267.67 |
|  | 272.53 |
|  | 277.40 |
|  | 282.27 |
|  | 287.13 |
|  | 292.00 |

| £ | $ c. | £ | $ c. | £ | $ c. |
|---|---|---|---|---|---|
| 61... | 296.87 | 98... | 476.93 | 135... | 657.00 |
| 62... | 301.73 | 99... | 481.80 | 136... | 661.87 |
| 63... | 306.60 | 100... | 486.67 | 137... | 666.73 |
| 64... | 311.47 | 101... | 491.53 | 138... | 671.60 |
| 65... | 316.33 | 102... | 496.40 | 139... | 676.47 |
| 66... | 321.20 | 103... | 501.27 | 140... | 681.33 |
| 67... | 326.07 | 104... | 506.13 | 141... | 686.20 |
| 68... | 330.93 | 105... | 511.00 | 142... | 691.07 |
| 69... | 335.80 | 106... | 515.87 | 143... | 695.93 |
| 70... | 340.67 | 107... | 520.73 | 144... | 700.80 |
| 71... | 345.53 | 108... | 525.60 | 145... | 705.67 |
| 72... | 350.40 | 109... | 530.47 | 146... | 710.53 |
| 73... | 355.27 | 110... | 535.33 | 147... | 715.40 |
| 74... | 360.13 | 111... | 540.20 | 148... | 720.27 |
| 75... | 365.00 | 112... | 545.07 | 149... | 725.13 |
| 76... | 369.87 | 113... | 549.93 | 150... | 730.00 |
| 77... | 374.73 | 114... | 554.80 | 151... | 734.87 |
| 78... | 379.60 | 115... | 559.67 | 152... | 739.73 |
| 79... | 384.47 | 116... | 564.53 | 153... | 744.60 |
| 80... | 389.33 | 117... | 569.40 | 154... | 749.47 |
| 81... | 394.20 | 118... | 574.27 | 155... | 754.33 |
| 82... | 399.07 | 119... | 579.13 | 156... | 759.20 |
| 83... | 403.93 | 120... | 584.00 | 157... | 764.07 |
| 84... | 408.80 | 121... | 588.87 | 158... | 768.93 |
| 85... | 413.67 | 122... | 593.73 | 159... | 773.80 |
| 86... | 418.53 | 123... | 598.60 | 160... | 778.67 |
| 87... | 423.40 | 124... | 603.47 | 161... | 783.53 |
| 88... | 428.27 | 125... | 608.33 | 162... | 788.40 |
| 89... | 433.13 | 126... | 613.20 | 163... | 793.27 |
| 90... | 438.00 | 127... | 618.07 | 164... | 798.13 |
| 91... | 442.87 | 128... | 622.93 | 165... | 803.00 |
| 92... | 447.73 | 129... | 627.80 | 166... | 807.87 |
| 93... | 452.60 | 130... | 632.67 | 167... | 812.73 |
| 94... | 457.47 | 131... | 637.53 | 168... | 817.60 |
| 95... | 462.33 | 132... | 642.40 | 169... | 822.47 |
| 96... | 467.20 | 133... | 647.27 | 170... | 827.33 |
| 97... | 472.07 | 134... | 652.13 | 171... | 832.20 |

| £ | $ c. | £ | $ c. | £ | $ c. |
|---|---|---|---|---|---|
| 172... | 837.07 | 209... | 1017.13 | 246... | 1197.20 |
| 173... | 841.93 | 210... | 1022.00 | 247... | 1202.07 |
| 174... | 846.80 | 211... | 1026.87 | 248... | 1206.93 |
| 175... | 851.67 | 212... | 1031.73 | 249... | 1211.80 |
| 176... | 856.53 | 213... | 1036.60 | 250... | 1216.67 |
| 177... | 861.40 | 214... | 1041.47 | 251... | 1221.53 |
| 178... | 866.27 | 215... | 1046.33 | 252... | 1226.40 |
| 179... | 871.13 | 216... | 1051.20 | 253... | 1231.27 |
| 180... | 876.00 | 217... | 1056.07 | 254... | 1236.13 |
| 181... | 880.87 | 218... | 1060.93 | 255... | 1241.00 |
| 182... | 885.73 | 219... | 1065.80 | 256... | 1245.87 |
| 183... | 890.60 | 220... | 1070.67 | 257... | 1250.73 |
| 184... | 895.47 | 221... | 1075.53 | 258... | 1255.60 |
| 185... | 900.33 | 222... | 1080.40 | 259... | 1260.47 |
| 186... | 905.20 | 223... | 1085.27 | 260... | 1265.33 |
| 187... | 910.07 | 224... | 1090.13 | 261... | 1270.20 |
| 188... | 914.93 | 225... | 1095.00 | 262... | 1275.07 |
| 189... | 919.80 | 226... | 1099.87 | 263... | 1279.93 |
| 190... | 924.67 | 227... | 1104.73 | 264... | 1284.80 |
| 191... | 929.53 | 228... | 1109.60 | 265... | 1289.67 |
| 192... | 934.40 | 229... | 1114.47 | 266... | 1294.53 |
| 193... | 939.27 | 230... | 1119.33 | 267... | 1299.40 |
| 194... | 944.13 | 231... | 1124.20 | 268... | 1304.27 |
| 195... | 949.00 | 232... | 1129.07 | 269... | 1309.13 |
| 196... | 953.87 | 233... | 1133.93 | 270... | 1314.00 |
| 197... | 958.73 | 234... | 1138.80 | 271... | 1318.87 |
| 198... | 963.60 | 235... | 1143.67 | 272... | 1323.73 |
| 199... | 968.47 | 236... | 1148.53 | 273... | 1328.60 |
| 200... | 973.33 | 237... | 1153.40 | 274... | 1333.47 |
| 201... | 978.20 | 238... | 1158.27 | 275... | 1338.33 |
| 202... | 983.07 | 239... | 1163.13 | 276... | 1343.20 |
| 203... | 987.93 | 240... | 1168.00 | 277... | 1348.07 |
| 204... | 992.80 | 241... | 1172.87 | 278... | 1352.93 |
| 205... | 997.67 | 242... | 1177.73 | 279... | 1357.80 |
| 206... | 1002.53 | 243... | 1182.60 | 280... | 1362.67 |
| 207... | 1007.40 | 244... | 1187.47 | 281... | 1367.53 |
| 208... | 1012.27 | 245... | 1192.33 | 282... | 1372.40 |

| $ c. | £ | $ c. | £ | $ c. |
|---|---|---|---|---|
| .. 1377.27 | 320... | 1557.33 | 357... | 1737.40 |
| .. 1382.13 | 321... | 1562.20 | 358... | 1742.27 |
| .. 1387.00 | 322... | 1567.07 | 359... | 1747.13 |
| .. 1391.87 | 323... | 1571.93 | 360... | 1752.00 |
| .. 1396.73 | 324... | 1576.80 | 361... | 1756.87 |
| .. 1401.60 | 325... | 1581.67 | 362... | 1761.73 |
| .. 1406.47 | 326... | 1586.53 | 363... | 1766.60 |
| .. 1411.33 | 327... | 1591.40 | 364... | 1771.47 |
| .. 1416.20 | 328... | 1596.27 | 365... | 1776.33 |
| .. 1421.07 | 329... | 1601.13 | 366... | 1781.20 |
| .. 1425.93 | 330... | 1606.00 | 367... | 1786.07 |
| .. 1430.80 | 331... | 1610.87 | 368... | 1790.93 |
| .. 1435.67 | 332... | 1615.73 | 369... | 1795.80 |
| .. 1440.53 | 333... | 1620.60 | 370... | 1800.67 |
| .. 1445.40 | 334... | 1625.47 | 371... | 1805.53 |
| .. 1450.27 | 335... | 1630.33 | 372... | 1810.40 |
| .. 1455.13 | 336... | 1635.20 | 373... | 1815.27 |
| .. 1460.00 | 337... | 1640.07 | 374... | 1820.13 |
| .. 1464.87 | 338... | 1644.93 | 375... | 1825.00 |
| .. 1469.73 | 339... | 1649.80 | 376... | 1829.87 |
| .. 1474.60 | 340... | 1654.67 | 377... | 1834.73 |
| .. 1479.47 | 341... | 1659.53 | 378... | 1839.60 |
| .. 1484.33 | 342... | 1664.40 | 379... | 1844.47 |
| .. 1489.20 | 343... | 1669.27 | 380... | 1849.33 |
| .. 1494.07 | 344... | 1674.13 | 381... | 1854 20 |
| .. 1498.93 | 345... | 1679.00 | 382... | 1859.07 |
| .. 1503.80 | 346... | 1683.87 | 383... | 1863.93 |
| .. 1508.67 | 347... | 1688.73 | 384... | 1868.80 |
| .. 1513.53 | 348... | 1693.60 | 385... | 1873.67 |
| .. 1518.40 | 349.. | 1698.47 | 386... | 1878.53 |
| .. 1523.27 | 350... | 1702.33 | 387... | 1883.40 |
| .. 1528.13 | 351... | 1708.20 | 388... | 1888.27 |
| .. 1533.00 | 352... | 1713.07 | 389... | 1893.13 |
| .. 1537.87 | 353... | 1717.93 | 390... | 1898.00 |
| .. 1542.73 | 354... | 1722.80 | 391... | 1902.87 |
| .. 1547.60 | 355... | 1727.67 | 392... | 1907.73 |
| .. 1552.47 | 356... | 1732.53 | 393... | 1912.60 |

| £ | $ c. | £ | $ c. | £ | $ |
|---|---|---|---|---|---|
| 394... | 1917.47 | 431... | 2097.53 | 468... | 2277.6 |
| 395... | 1922.33 | 432... | 2102.40 | 469... | 2282.4 |
| 396... | 1927.20 | 433... | 2107.27 | 470... | 2287.3 |
| 397... | 1932.07 | 434... | 2112.13 | 471... | 2292.2 |
| 398... | 1936.93 | 435... | 2117.00 | 472... | 2297.0 |
| 399... | 1941.80 | 436... | 2121.87 | 473... | 2301.9 |
| 400... | 1946.67 | 437... | 2126.73 | 474... | 2306.8 |
| 401... | 1951.53 | 438... | 2131.60 | 475... | 2311.6 |
| 402... | 1956.40 | 439... | 2136.47 | 476... | 2316.5 |
| 403... | 1961.27 | 440... | 2141.33 | 477... | 2321.4 |
| 404... | 1966.13 | 441... | 2146.20 | 478... | 2326.2 |
| 405... | 1971.00 | 442... | 2151.07 | 479... | 2331.1 |
| 406... | 1975.87 | 443... | 2155.93 | 480... | 2336.0 |
| 407... | 1980.73 | 444... | 2160.80 | 481... | 2340.87 |
| 408... | 1985.60 | 445... | 2165.67 | 482... | 2345.73 |
| 409... | 1990.47 | 446... | 2170.53 | 483... | 2350.60 |
| 410... | 1995.33 | 447... | 2175.40 | 484... | 2355·47 |
| 411... | 2000.20 | 448... | 2180.27 | 485... | 2360.33 |
| 412... | 2005.07 | 449... | 2185.13 | 486... | 2365.20 |
| 413... | 2009.93 | 450... | 2190.00 | 487... | 2370.07 |
| 414... | 2014.80 | 451... | 2194.87 | 488... | 2374.93 |
| 415... | 2019.67 | 452... | 2199.73 | 489... | 2379.80 |
| 416... | 2024.53 | 453... | 2204.60 | 490... | 2384.67 |
| 417... | 2029.40 | 454... | 2209.47 | 491... | 2389.53 |
| 418... | 2034.27 | 455... | 2214.33 | 492... | 2394.40 |
| 419... | 2039.13 | 456... | 2219.20 | 493... | 2399.27 |
| 420... | 2044.00 | 457... | 2224.07 | 494... | 2404.13 |
| 421... | 2048.87 | 458... | 2228.93 | 495... | 2409.00 |
| 422... | 2053.73 | 459... | 2233.80 | 496... | 2413.87 |
| 423... | 2058.60 | 460... | 2238.67 | 497... | 2418.73 |
| 424... | 2063.47 | 461... | 2243.53 | 498... | 2423.60 |
| 425... | 2068.33 | 462... | 2248.40 | 499... | 2428.47 |
| 426... | 2073.20 | 463... | 2253.27 | 500... | 2433.33 |
| 427... | 2078.07 | 464... | 2258.13 | 501... | 2438.20 |
| 428... | 2082.93 | 465... | 2263.00 | 502... | 2443.07 |
| 429... | 2087.80 | 466... | 2267.87 | 503... | 2447.93 |
| 430... | 2092.67 | 467... | 2272.73 | 504... | 2452.80 |

| £ | $ c. | £ | $ c. | £ | $ c. |
|---|------|---|------|---|------|
| 505... | 2457.67 | 542... | 2637.73 | 579... | 2817.80 |
| 506... | 2462.53 | 543... | 2642.6C | 580... | 2822.67 |
| 507... | 2467.40 | 544... | 2647.47 | 581... | 2827.53 |
| 508... | 2472.27 | 545... | 2652.33 | 582... | 2832.40 |
| 509... | 2477.13 | 546... | 2657.20 | 583... | 2837.27 |
| 510... | 2482.00 | 547... | 2662.07 | 584... | 2842.13 |
| 511... | 2486.87 | 548... | 2666.93 | 585... | 2847.00 |
| 512... | 2491.73 | 549... | 2671.80 | 586... | 2851.87 |
| 513... | 2496.60 | 550... | 2676.67 | 587... | 2856.73 |
| 514... | 2501.47 | 551... | 2681.53 | 588... | 2861.60 |
| 515... | 2506.33 | 552... | 2686.40 | 589... | 2866.47 |
| 516... | 2511.20 | 553... | 2691.27 | 590... | 2871.33 |
| 517... | 2516.07 | 554... | 2696.13 | 591... | 2876.20 |
| 518... | 2520.93 | 555... | 2701.00 | 592... | 2881.07 |
| 519... | 2525.80 | 556... | 2705.87 | 593... | 2885.93 |
| 520... | 2530.67 | 557... | 2710.73 | 594... | 2890.80 |
| 521... | 2535.53 | 558... | 2715.60 | 595... | 2895.67 |
| 522... | 2540.40 | 559... | 2720.47 | 596... | 2900.53 |
| 523... | 2545.27 | 560... | 2725.33 | 597... | 2905.40 |
| 524... | 2550.13 | 561... | 2730.20 | 598... | 2910.27 |
| 525... | 2555.00 | 562... | 2735.07 | 599... | 2915.13 |
| 526... | 2559.87 | 563... | 2739.93 | 600... | 2920.00 |
| 527... | 2564.73 | 564... | 2744.80 | 601... | 2924.87 |
| 528... | 2569.60 | 565... | 2749.67 | 602... | 2929.73 |
| 529... | 2574.47 | 566... | 2754.53 | 603... | 2934.60 |
| 530... | 2579.33 | 567... | 2759.40 | 604... | 2939.47 |
| 531... | 2584.20 | 568... | 2764.27 | 605... | 2944.33 |
| 532... | 2589.07 | 569... | 2769.13 | 606... | 2949.20 |
| 533... | 2593.93 | 570... | 2774.00 | 607... | 2954.07 |
| 534... | 2598.80 | 571... | 2778.87 | 608... | 2958.93 |
| 535... | 2603.67 | 572... | 2783.73 | 609... | 2963.80 |
| 536... | 2608.53 | 573... | 2788.60 | 610... | 2968.67 |
| 537... | 2613.40 | 574... | 2793.47 | 611... | 2973.53 |
| 538... | 2618.27 | 575... | 2798.33 | 612... | 2978.40 |
| 539... | 2623.13 | 576... | 2803.20 | 613... | 2983.27 |
| 540... | 2628 00 | 577... | 2808.07 | 614... | 2988.13 |
| 541... | 2632.87 | 578... | 2812.93 | 615... | 2993.60 |

| £ | $ c. | £ | $ c | £ | $ | £ | |
|---|---|---|---|---|---|---|---|
| 616... | 2997.87 | 653... | 3177.93 | 690... | 3358.0 | 727... | 3 |
| 617... | 3002.73 | 654... | 3182.80 | 691... | 3362.8 | 728... | 3 |
| 618... | 3007.60 | 655... | 3187.67 | 692... | 3367.7 | 729... | 3 |
| 619... | 3012.47 | 656... | 3192.53 | 693... | 3372.6 | 730... | 3 |
| 620... | 3017.33 | 657... | 3197.40 | 694... | 3377.4 | 731... | 3 |
| 621... | 3022.20 | 658... | 3202.27 | 695... | 3382.3 | 732... | 3 |
| 622... | 3027.07 | 659... | 3207.13 | 696... | 3387.2 | 733... | 3 |
| 623... | 3031.93 | 660... | 3212.00 | 697... | 3392.0 | 734... | 3 |
| 624... | 3036.80 | 661... | 3216.87 | 698... | 3396.9 | 735... | 3 |
| 625... | 3041.67 | 662... | 3221.73 | 699... | 3401.8 | 736... | 3 |
| 626... | 3046.53 | 663... | 3226.60 | 700... | 3406.6 | 737... | 3 |
| 627... | 3051.40 | 664... | 3231.47 | 701... | 3411.5 | 738... | 3 |
| 628... | 3056.27 | 665... | 3236.33 | 702... | 3416.4 | 739... | 3 |
| 629... | 3061.13 | 666... | 3241.20 | 703... | 3421.27 | 740... | 3 |
| 630... | 3066.00 | 667... | 3246.07 | 704... | 3426.13 | 741... | 3 |
| 631... | 3070.87 | 668... | 3250.93 | 705... | 3431.00 | 742... | 3 |
| 632... | 3075.73 | 669... | 3255.80 | 706... | 3435.87 | 743... | 3 |
| 633... | 3080.60 | 670... | 3260.67 | 707... | 3440.73 | 744... | 3 |
| 634... | 3085.47 | 671... | 3265.53 | 708... | 3445.60 | 745... | 3 |
| 635... | 3090.33 | 672... | 3270.40 | 709... | 3450.47 | 746... |  |
| 636... | 3095.20 | 673... | 3275.27 | 710... | 3455.33 | 747... |  |
| 637... | 3100.07 | 674... | 3280.13 | 711... | 3460.20 | 748... |  |
| 638... | 3104.93 | 675... | 3285.00 | 712... | 3465.07 | 749... |  |
| 639... | 3109.80 | 676... | 3289.87 | 713... | 3469.93 | 750... |  |
| 640... | 3114.67 | 677... | 3294.73 | 714... | 3474.80 | 751... |  |
| 641... | 3119.53 | 678... | 3299.60 | 715... | 3479.67 | 752... |  |
| 642... | 3124.40 | 679... | 3304.47 | 716... | 3484.53 | 753... |  |
| 643... | 3129.27 | 680... | 3309.33 | 717... | 3489.40 | 754... |  |
| 644... | 3134.13 | 681... | 3314.20 | 718... | 3494.27 | 755... |  |
| 645... | 3139.00 | 682... | 3319.07 | 719... | 3499.13 | 756... |  |
| 646... | 3143.87 | 683... | 3323.93 | 720... | 3504.00 | 757... |  |
| 647... | 3148.73 | 684... | 3328.80 | 721... | 3508.87 | 758... |  |
| 648... | 3153.60 | 685... | 3333.67 | 722... | 3513.73 | 759... |  |
| 649... | 3158.47 | 686... | 3338.53 | 723... | 3518.60 | 760... |  |
| 650... | 3163.33 | 687... | 3343.40 | 724... | 3523.47 | 761... |  |
| 651... | 3168.20 | 688... | 3348.27 | 725... | 3528.33 | 762... |  |
| 652... | 3173.07 | 689... | 3353.13 | 726... | 3533.20 | 763... |  |

| $ c. | £ | $ c. | £ | $ c |
|---|---|---|---|---|
| .. 3538.07 | 764... | 3718.13 | 801... | 3898.20 |
| .. 3542.93 | 765... | 3723.00 | 802... | 3903.07 |
| .. 3547.80 | 766... | 3727.87 | 803... | 3907.93 |
| .. 3552.07 | 767... | 3732.73 | 804... | 3912.80 |
| .. 3557.73 | 768... | 3737.60 | 805... | 3917.67 |
| .. 3562.40 | 769... | 3742.47 | 806... | 3922.53 |
| .. 3567.27 | 770... | 3747.33 | 807... | 3927.40 |
| .. 3572.13 | 771... | 3752.20 | 808... | 3932.27 |
| .. 3577.00 | 772... | 3757.07 | 809... | 3937.13 |
| .. 3581.87 | 773... | 3761.93 | 810... | 3942.00 |
| .. 3586:73 | 774... | 3766.80 | 811... | 3946.87 |
| .. 3591.60 | 775... | 3771.67 | 812... | 3951.73 |
| .. 3596.47 | 776... | 3776.53 | 813... | 3956.60 |
| .. 3601.33 | 777... | 3781.40 | 814... | 3961.47 |
| .. 3606.20 | 778... | 3786.27 | 815... | 3966.33 |
| .. 3611.07 | 779... | 3791.13 | 816... | 3971.20 |
| .. 3615.93 | 780... | 3796.00 | 817... | 3976.07 |
| .. 3620.80 | 781... | 3800.87 | 818... | 3980.93 |
| .. 3625.67 | 782... | 3805.73 | 819... | 3985.80 |
| .. 3630.53 | 783... | 3810.60 | 820... | 3990.67 |
| .. 3635.40 | 784... | 3815.47 | 821... | 3995.53 |
| .. 3640.27 | 785... | 3820.33 | 822... | 4000.40 |
| .. 3645.13 | 786... | 3825.20 | 823... | 4005.27 |
| .. 3650.00 | 787... | 3830.07 | 824... | 4010.13 |
| .. 3654.87 | 788... | 3834.93 | 825... | 4015.00 |
| .. 3659.73 | 789... | 3839.80 | 826... | 4019.87 |
| .. 3664.60 | 790... | 3844.67 | 827... | 4024.73 |
| .. 3669.47 | 791... | 3849.53 | 828... | 4029.60 |
| .. 3674.33 | 792... | 3854.40 | 829... | 4034.47 |
| .. 3679.20 | 793... | 3859.27 | 830... | 4039.33 |
| .. 3684.07 | 794... | 3864.13 | 831... | 4044.20 |
| .. 3688.93 | 795... | 3869.00 | 832... | 4049.07 |
| .. 3693.80 | 796... | 3873.87 | 833... | 4053.93 |
| .. 3698.67 | 797... | 3878.73 | 834... | 4058.80 |
| .. 3703.53 | 798... | 3883.60 | 835... | 4063.67 |
| .. 3708.40 | 799... | 3888.47 | 836... | 4068.53 |
| .. 3713.27 | 800... | 3893.33 | 837... | 4073.40 |

| £ | $ c. | £ | $ c. | £ | $ c. |
|---|---|---|---|---|---|
| 838... | 4078.27 | 875... | 4258.33 | 912... | 4438.40 |
| 839... | 4083.13 | 876... | 4263.20 | 913... | 4443.27 |
| 840... | 4088.00 | 877... | 4268.07 | 914... | 4448.13 |
| 841... | 4092.87 | 878... | 4272.93 | 915... | 4453.00 |
| 842... | 4097.73 | 879... | 4277.80 | 916... | 4457.87 |
| 843... | 4102.60 | 880... | 4282.67 | 917... | 4462.73 |
| 844... | 4107.47 | 881... | 4287.53 | 918... | 4467.60 |
| 845... | 4112.33 | 882... | 4292.40 | 919... | 4472.47 |
| 846... | 4117.20 | 883... | 4297.27 | 920... | 4477.33 |
| 847... | 4122.07 | 884... | 4302.13 | 921... | 4482.20 |
| 848... | 4126.93 | 885... | 4307.00 | 922... | 4487.07 |
| 849... | 4131.80 | 886... | 4311.87 | 923... | 4491.93 |
| 850... | 4136.67 | 887... | 4316.73 | 924... | 4496.80 |
| 851... | 4141.53 | 888... | 4321.60 | 925... | 4501.67 |
| 852... | 4146.40 | 889... | 4326.47 | 926... | 4506.53 |
| 853... | 4151.27 | 890... | 4331.33 | 927... | 4511.40 |
| 854... | 4156.13 | 891... | 4336.20 | 928... | 4516.27 |
| 855... | 4161.00 | 892... | 4341.07 | 929... | 4521.13 |
| 856... | 4165.87 | 893... | 4345.93 | 930... | 4526.00 |
| 857... | 4170.73 | 894... | 4350.80 | 931... | 4530.87 |
| 858... | 4175.60 | 895... | 4355.67 | 932... | 4535.73 |
| 859... | 4180.47 | 896... | 4360.53 | 933... | 4540.60 |
| 860... | 4185.33 | 897... | 4365.40 | 934... | 4545.47 |
| 861... | 4190.20 | 898... | 4370.27 | 935... | 4550.33 |
| 862... | 4195.07 | 899... | 4375.13 | 936... | 4555.20 |
| 863... | 4199.93 | 900... | 4380.00 | 937... | 4560.07 |
| 864... | 4204.80 | 901... | 4384.87 | 938... | 4564.93 |
| 865... | 4209.67 | 902... | 4389.73 | 939... | 4569.80 |
| 866... | 4214.53 | 903... | 4394.60 | 940... | 4574.67 |
| 867... | 4219.40 | 904... | 4399.47 | 941... | 4579.53 |
| 868... | 4224.27 | 905... | 4404.33 | 942... | 4584.40 |
| 869... | 4229.13 | 906... | 4409.20 | 943... | 4589.27 |
| 870... | 4234.00 | 907... | 4414.07 | 944... | 4594.13 |
| 871... | 4238.87 | 908... | 4418.93 | 945... | 4599.00 |
| 872... | 4243.73 | 909... | 4423.80 | 946... | 4603.87 |
| 873... | 4248.60 | 910... | 4428.67 | 947... | 4608.73 |
| 874... | 4253.47 | 911... | 4433.53 | 948... | 4613.60 |

| $ c. | £ | $ c. | £ | $ c. | £ | $ c. |
|---|---|---|---|---|---|---|
| ... 4438.40 | 949... | 4618.47 | 973... | 4735.27 | 997... | 4852.07 |
| ... 4443.27 | 950... | 4623.33 | 974... | 4740.13 | 998... | 4856.93 |
| ... 4448.13 | 951... | 4628.20 | 975... | 4745.00 | 999... | 4861.80 |
| .. 4453.00 | 952... | 4633.07 | 976... | 4749.87 | 1000... | 4866.67 |
| .. 4457.87 | 953... | 4637.93 | 977... | 4754.73 | 1100... | 5353.33 |
| .. 4462.73 | 954... | 4642.80 | 978... | 4759.60 | 1200... | 5840.00 |
| .. 4467.60 | 955... | 4647.67 | 979... | 4764.47 | 1300... | 6326.67 |
| .. 4472.47 | 956... | 4652.53 | 980... | 4769.33 | 1400... | 6813.33 |
| .. 4477.33 | 957... | 4657.40 | 981... | 4774.20 | 1500... | 7300.00 |
| .. 4482.20 | 958... | 4662.27 | 982... | 4779.07 | 1600... | 7786.67 |
| .. 4487.07 | 959... | 4667.13 | 983... | 4783.93 | 1700... | 8273.33 |
| . 4491.93 | 960... | 4672.00 | 984... | 4788.80 | 1800... | 8760.00 |
| . 4496.80 | 961... | 4676.87 | 985... | 4793.67 | 1900... | 9246.67 |
| . 4501.67 | 962... | 4681.73 | 986... | 4798.53 | 2000... | 9733.33 |
| . 4506.53 | 963... | 4686.60 | 987... | 4803.40 | 3000... | 14600.00 |
| . 4511.40 | 964... | 4691.47 | 988... | 4808.27 | 4000... | 19466.67 |
| . 4516.27 | 965... | 4696.33 | 989... | 4813.13 | 5000... | 24333.33 |
| . 4521.13 | 966... | 4701.20 | 990... | 4818.00 | 6000... | 29200.00 |
| . 4526.00 | 967... | 4706.07 | 991... | 4822.87 | 7000... | 34066.67 |
| 4530.87 | 968... | 4710.93 | 992... | 4827.73 | 8000... | 38933.33 |
| 4535.73 | 969... | 4715.80 | 993... | 4832.60 | 9000... | 43800.00 |
| 4540.60 | 970... | 4720.67 | 994... | 4837.47 | 10000... | 48666.67 |
| 4545.47 | 971... | 4725.53 | 995... | 4842.33 | 50000... | 243333.33 |
| 4550.33 | 972... | 4730.40 | 996... | 4847.20 | | |
| 4555.20 | | | | | | |
| 4560.07 | | | | | | |
| 4564.93 | | | | | | |
| 4569.80 | | | | | | |
| 4574.67 | | | | | | |
| 4579.53 | | | | | | |
| 4584.40 | | | | | | |
| 4589.27 | | | | | | |
| 4594.13 | | | | | | |
| 4599.00 | | | | | | |
| 4603.87 | | | | | | |
| 4608.73 | | | | | | |
| 4613.60 | | | | | | |

| PENCE. | | SHILLINGS. | | SHILLINGS. | |
|---|---|---|---|---|---|
| 1... | 2 | 1... | .24$\frac{1}{3}$ | 13... | 3.16$\frac{1}{3}$ |
| 2... | 4 | 2... | .48$\frac{2}{3}$ | 14... | 3.40$\frac{2}{3}$ |
| 3... | 6 | 3... | .73 | 15... | 3.65 |
| 4... | 8 | 4... | .97$\frac{1}{3}$ | 16... | 3.89$\frac{1}{3}$ |
| 5... | 10 | 5... | 1.21$\frac{2}{3}$ | 17... | 4.13$\frac{2}{3}$ |
| 6... | 12 | 6... | 1.46 | 18... | 4.38 |
| 7... | 14 | 7... | 1.70$\frac{1}{3}$ | 19... | 4.62 |
| 8... | 16 | 8... | 1.94$\frac{2}{3}$ | 20... | 4.86$\frac{2}{3}$ |
| 9... | 18 | 9... | 2.19 | | |
| 10... | 20 | 10... | 2.43$\frac{1}{3}$ | | |
| 11... | 22 | 11... | 2.67$\frac{2}{3}$ | | |
| 12... | 24$\frac{1}{3}$ | 12... | 2.92 | | |

F

# FRANCS

REDUCED TO

# DOLLARS AND CENTS.

## 1 FRANC EQUAL TO 19⅕ CENTS.

| F. | $ c. | F. | $ c. | F. | $ c. |
|---|---|---|---|---|---|
| 1... | .19 | 25... | 4.83 | 49... | 9.46 |
| 2... | .39 | 26... | 5.02 | 50... | 9.65 |
| 3... | .58 | 27... | 5.21 | 51... | 9.84 |
| 4... | .77 | 28... | 5.40 | 52... | 10.04 |
| 5... | .97 | 29... | 5.60 | 53... | 10.23 |
| 6... | 1.16 | 30... | 5.79 | 54... | 10.42 |
| 7... | 1.35 | 31... | 5.98 | 55... | 10.62 |
| 8... | 1.54 | 32... | 6.18 | 56... | 10.81 |
| 9... | 1.74 | 33... | 6.37 | 57... | 11.00 |
| 10... | 1.93 | 34... | 6.56 | 58... | 11.19 |
| 11... | 2.12 | 35... | 6.76 | 59... | 11.39 |
| 12... | 2.32 | 36... | 6.95 | 60... | 11.58 |
| 13... | 2.51 | 37... | 7.14 | 61... | 11.77 |
| 14... | 2.70 | 38... | 7.33 | 62... | 11.97 |
| 15... | 2.90 | 39... | 7.53 | 63... | 12.16 |
| 16... | 3.09 | 40... | 7.72 | 64... | 12.35 |
| 17... | 3.28 | 41... | 7.91 | 65... | 12.55 |
| 18... | 3.47 | 42... | 8.11 | 66... | 12.74 |
| 19... | 3.67 | 43... | 8.30 | 67... | 12.93 |
| 20... | 3.86 | 44... | 8.49 | 68... | 13.12 |
| 21... | 4.05 | 45... | 8.69 | 69... | 13.32 |
| 22... | 4.25 | 46... | 8.88 | 70... | 13.51 |
| 23... | 4.44 | 47... | 9.07 | 71.. | 13.70 |
| 24... | 4.63 | 48... | 9.26 | 72... | 13.90 |

| F. | $ C. | F. | $ C. | F. | $ C. |
|---|---|---|---|---|---|
| 73... | 14.09 | 110... | 21.23 | 147... | 28.37 |
| 74... | 14.28 | 111... | 21.42 | 148... | 28.56 |
| 75... | 14.48 | 112... | 21.62 | 149... | 28.76 |
| 76... | 14.67 | 113... | 21.81 | 150... | 28.95 |
| 77... | 14.86 | 114... | 22.00 | 151... | 29.14 |
| 78... | 15.05 | 115... | 22.20 | 152... | 29.34 |
| 79... | 15.25 | 116... | 22.39 | 153... | 29.53 |
| 80... | 15.44 | 117... | 22.58 | 154... | 29.72 |
| 81... | 15.63 | 118... | 22.77 | 155... | 29.92 |
| 82... | 15.83 | 119... | 22.97 | 156... | 30.11 |
| 83... | 16.02 | 120... | 23.16 | 157... | 30.30 |
| 84... | 16.21 | 121... | 23.35 | 158... | 30.49 |
| 85... | 16.41 | 122... | 23.55 | 159... | 30.69 |
| 86... | 16.60 | 123... | 23.74 | 160... | 30.88 |
| 87... | 16.79 | 124... | 23.93 | 161... | 31.07 |
| 88... | 16.98 | 125... | 24.13 | 162... | 31.27 |
| 89... | 17.18 | 126... | 24.32 | 163... | 31.46 |
| 90... | 17.37 | 127... | 24.51 | 164... | 31.65 |
| 91... | 17.56 | 128... | 24.70 | 165... | 31.85 |
| 92... | 17.76 | 129... | 24.90 | 166... | 32.04 |
| 93... | 17.95 | 130... | 25.09 | 167... | 32.23 |
| 94... | 18.14 | 131... | 25.28 | 168... | 32.42 |
| 95... | 18.34 | 132... | 25.48 | 169... | 32.62 |
| 96... | 18.53 | 133... | 25.67 | 170... | 32.81 |
| 97... | 18.72 | 134... | 25.86 | 171... | 33.00 |
| 98... | 18.91 | 135... | 26.06 | 172... | 33.20 |
| 99... | 19.11 | 136... | 26.25 | 173... | 33.39 |
| 100... | 19.30 | 137... | 26.44 | 174... | 33.58 |
| 101... | 19.49 | 138... | 26.63 | 175... | 33.78 |
| 102... | 19.69 | 139... | 26.83 | 176... | 33.97 |
| 103... | 19.88 | 140... | 27.02 | 177... | 34.16 |
| 104... | 20.07 | 141... | 27.21 | 178... | 34.35 |
| 105... | 20.27 | 142... | 27.41 | 179... | 34.55 |
| 106... | 20.46 | 143... | 27.60 | 180... | 34.74 |
| 107... | 20.65 | 144... | 27.79 | 181... | 34.93 |
| 108... | 20.84 | 145... | 27.99 | 182... | 35.13 |
| 109... | 21.04 | 146... | 28.18 | 183... | 35.32 |

| F. | $ c. | F. | $ c. | F. | $ c. |
|---|---|---|---|---|---|
| 184... | 35.51 | 221... | 42.65 | 258... | 49.79 |
| 185... | 35.71 | 222... | 42.85 | 259... | 49.99 |
| 186... | 35.90 | 223... | 43.04 | 260... | 50.18 |
| 187... | 36.09 | 224... | 43.23 | 261... | 50.37 |
| 188... | 36 28 | 225... | 43.43 | 262... | 50.57 |
| 189... | 36.48 | 226... | 43.62 | 263... | 50.76 |
| 190... | 36.67 | 227... | 43.81 | 264... | 50.95 |
| 191... | 36.86 | 228... | 44.00 | 265... | 51.15 |
| 192... | 37.06 | 229... | 44.20 | 266... | 51.34 |
| 193... | 37.25 | 230... | 44.39 | 267... | 51.53 |
| 194... | 37.44 | 231... | 44.58 | 268... | 51.72 |
| 195... | 37.64 | 232... | 44.78 | 269... | 51.92 |
| 196... | 37.83 | 233... | 44.97 | 270... | 52.11 |
| 197... | 38.02 | 234... | 45.16 | 271... | 52.30 |
| 198... | 38.21 | 235... | 45.36 | 272... | 52.50 |
| 199... | 38.41 | 236... | 45.55 | 273... | 52·69 |
| 200... | 38.60 | 237... | 45.74 | 274... | 52.88 |
| 201. . | 38.79 | 238... | 45.93 | 275... | 53.08 |
| 202... | 38.99 | 239... | 46.13 | 276... | 53·27 |
| 203... | 39.18 | 240... | 46.32 | 277... | 53.46 |
| 204... | 39.37 | 241... | 46.51 | 278... | 53.65 |
| 205... | 39.57 | 242... | 46.71 | 279... | 53.85 |
| 206... | 39.76 | 243... | 46.90 | 280... | 54.04 |
| 207... | 39.95 | 244... | 47.09 | 281... | 54.23 |
| 208... | 40.14 | 245... | 47.29 | 282... | 54.43 |
| 209... | 40.34 | 246... | 47.48 | 283... | 54.62 |
| 210... | 40.53 | 247... | 47.67 | 284... | 54.81 |
| 211... | 40.72 | 248... | 47.86 | 285... | 55.01 |
| 212... | 40.92 | 249... | 48.06 | 286... | 55.20 |
| 213... | 41.11 | 250... | 48.25 | 287... | 55.39 |
| 214... | 41.30 | 251... | 48.44 | 288... | 55.58 |
| 215... | 41.50 | 252... | 48.64 | 289... | 55.78 |
| 216... | 41.69 | 253... | 48.83 | 290... | 55.97 |
| 217... | 41.88 | 254... | 49.02 | 291... | 56.16 |
| 218... | 42.07 | 255... | 49.22 | 292... | 56.36 |
| 219... | 42.27 | 256... | 49.41 | 293... | 56.55 |
| 220... | 42.46 | 257... | 49.60 | 294... | 56.74 |

| $ C. | F. | $ C. | F. | $ C. | F. | $ C. |
|---|---|---|---|---|---|---|
| ... 49.79 | 295... | 56.94 | 332... | 64.08 | 369... | 71.22 |
| ... 49.99 | 296... | 57.13 | 333... | 64.27 | 370... | 71.41 |
| .. 50.18 | 297... | 57.32 | 334... | 64.46 | 371... | 71.60 |
| .. 50.37 | 298... | 57.51 | 335... | 64.66 | 372... | 71.80 |
| .. 50.57 | 299... | 57.71 | 336... | 64.85 | 373... | 71.99 |
| .. 50.76 | 300... | 57.90 | 337... | 65.04 | 374... | 72.18 |
| .. 50.95 | 301... | 58.09 | 338... | 65.23 | 375... | 72.38 |
| .. 51.15 | 302... | 58.29 | 339... | 65.43 | 376... | 72.57 |
| . 51.34 | 303... | 58.48 | 340... | 65.62 | 377... | 72.76 |
| . 51.53 | 304... | 58.67 | 341... | 65.81 | 378... | 72.95 |
| . 51.72 | 305... | 58.87 | 342... | 66.01 | 379... | 73.15 |
| . 51.92 | 306... | 59.06 | 343... | 66.20 | 380... | 73.34 |
| . 52.11 | 307... | 59.25 | 344... | 66.39 | 381... | 73.53 |
| . 52.30 | 308... | 59.44 | 345... | 66.59 | 382... | 73.73 |
| 52.50 | 309... | 59.64 | 346... | 66.78 | 383... | 73.92 |
| 52.69 | 310... | 59.83 | 347... | 66.97 | 384... | 74.11 |
| 52.88 | 311... | 60.02 | 348... | 67.16 | 385... | 74.31 |
| 53.08 | 312... | 60.22 | 349... | 67.36 | 386... | 74.50 |
| 53.27 | 313... | 60.41 | 350... | 67.55 | 387... | 74.69 |
| 53.46 | 314... | 60.60 | 351... | 67.74 | 388... | 74.88 |
| 53.65 | 315... | 60.80 | 352... | 67.94 | 389... | 75.08 |
| 53.85 | 316... | 60.99 | 353... | 68.13 | 390... | 75.27 |
| 54.04 | 317... | 61.18 | 354... | 68.32 | 391... | 75.46 |
| 54.23 | 318... | 61.37 | 355... | 68.52 | 392... | 75.66 |
| 54.43 | 319... | 61.57 | 356... | 68.71 | 393... | 75.85 |
| 54.62 | 320... | 61.76 | 357... | 68.90 | 394... | 76.04 |
| 54.81 | 321... | 61.95 | 358... | 69.09 | 395... | 76.24 |
| 55.01 | 322... | 62.15 | 359... | 69.29 | 396... | 76.43 |
| 55.20 | 323... | 62.34 | 360... | 69.48 | 397... | 76.62 |
| 55.39 | 324... | 62.53 | 361... | 69.67 | 398... | 76.81 |
| 55.58 | 325... | 62.73 | 362... | 69.87 | 399... | 77.01 |
| 55.78 | 326... | 62.92 | 363... | 70.06 | 400... | 77.20 |
| 55.97 | 327... | 63.11 | 364... | 70.25 | 401... | 77.39 |
| 56.16 | 328... | 63.30 | 365... | 70.45 | 402... | 77.59 |
| 56.36 | 329... | 63.50 | 366... | 70.64 | 403... | 77.78 |
| 56.55 | 330... | 63.69 | 367... | 70.83 | 404... | 77.97 |
| 56.74 | 331... | 63.88 | 368... | 71.02 | 405... | 78.17 |

| F. | $ c. | F. | $ c. | F. | $ c. |
|---|---|---|---|---|---|
| 406... | 78.36 | 443... | 85.50 | 480... | 92.64 |
| 407... | 78.55 | 444... | 85.69 | 481... | 92.83 |
| 408... | 78.74 | 445... | 85.89 | 482... | 93.03 |
| 409... | 78.94 | 446... | 86.08 | 483... | 93.22 |
| 410... | 79.13 | 447... | 86.27 | 484... | 93.41 |
| 411... | 79.32 | 448... | 86.46 | 485... | 93.61 |
| 412... | 79.52 | 449... | 86.66 | 486... | 93.80 |
| 413... | 79.71 | 450... | 86.85 | 487... | 93.99 |
| 414... | 79.90 | 451... | 87.04 | 488... | 94.18 |
| 415... | 80.10 | 452... | 87.24 | 489... | 94.38 |
| 416... | 80.29 | 453... | 87.43 | 490... | 94.57 |
| 417... | 80.48 | 454... | 87.62 | 491... | 94.76 |
| 418... | 80.67 | 455... | 87.82 | 492... | 94.96 |
| 419... | 80.87 | 456... | 88.01 | 493... | 95.15 |
| 420... | 81.06 | 457... | 88.20 | 494... | 95.34 |
| 421... | 81.25 | 458... | 88.39 | 495... | 95.54 |
| 422... | 81.45 | 459... | 88.59 | 496... | 95.73 |
| 423... | 81.64 | 460... | 88.78 | 497... | 95.92 |
| 424... | 81.83 | 461... | 88.97 | 498... | 96.11 |
| 425... | 82.03 | 462... | 89.17 | 499... | 96.31 |
| 426... | 82.22 | 463... | 89.36 | 500... | 96.50 |
| 427... | 82.41 | 464... | 89.55 | 501... | 96.69 |
| 428... | 82.60 | 465... | 89.75 | 502... | 96.39 |
| 429... | 82.80 | 466... | 89.94 | 503... | 97.08 |
| 430... | 82.99 | 467... | 90.13 | 504... | 97.27 |
| 431... | 83.18 | 468... | 90.32 | 505... | 97.47 |
| 432... | 83.38 | 469... | 90.52 | 506... | 97.66 |
| 433... | 83.57 | 470... | 90.71 | 507... | 97.85 |
| 434... | 83.76 | 471... | 90.90 | 508... | 98.04 |
| 435... | 83.96 | 472... | 91.10 | 509... | 98.24 |
| 436... | 84.15 | 473... | 91.29 | 510... | 98.43 |
| 437... | 84.34 | 474... | 91.48 | 511... | 98.62 |
| 438 . | 84.53 | 475... | 91.68 | 512... | 98.82 |
| 439... | 84.73 | 476... | 91.87 | 513... | 99.01 |
| 440... | 84.92 | 477... | 92.06 | 514... | 99.20 |
| 441... | 85.11 | 478... | 92.25 | 515... | 99.40 |
| 442... | 85.31 | 479... | 92.45 | 516... | 99.59 |

| $ c. | F. | $ c. | F. | $ c. | F. | $ c. |
|---|---|---|---|---|---|---|
| )... 92.64 | 517... | 99.78 | 554... | 106.92 | 591... | 114.06 |
| .... 92.83 | 518... | 99.97 | 555... | 107.12 | 592... | 114.26 |
| '... 93.03 | 519... | 100.17 | 556... | 107.31 | 593... | 114.45 |
| ... 93.22 | 520... | 100.36 | 557... 107.50 | | 594... | 114.64 |
| ... 93.41 | 521... | 100.55 | 558... | 107.69 | 595... | 114.84 |
| ... 93.61 | 522... | 100.75 | 559... | 107.89 | 596... | 115.03 |
| ... 93.80 | 523... | 100.94 | 560... | 108.08 | 597... | 115.22 |
| ... 93.99 | 524... | 101.13 | 561... | 108.27 | 598... | 115.41 |
| .. 94.18 | 525... | 101.33 | 562... | 108.47 | 599... | 115.61 |
| .. 94.38 | 526... | 101.52 | 563... | 108.66 | 600... | 115.80 |
| .. 94.57 | 527... | 101.71 | 564... | 108.85 | 601... | 115.99 |
| .. 94.76 | 528... | 101.90 | 565... | 109.05 | 602... | 116.19 |
| . 94.96 | 529... | 102.10 | 566... | 109.24 | 603... | 116.38 |
| . 95.15 | 530... | 102.29 | 567... | 109.43 | 604... | 116.57 |
| . 95.34 | 531... | 102.48 | 568... | 109.62 | 605... | 116.77 |
| . 95.54 | 532... | 102.68 | 569... | 109.82 | 606... | 116.96 |
| . 95.73 | 533... | 102.87 | 570... | 110.01 | 607... | 117.15 |
| 95.92 | 534... | 103.06 | 571... | 110.20 | 608... | 117.34 |
| 96.11 | 535... | 103.26 | 572... | 110.40 | 609... | 117.54 |
| 96.31 | 536... | 103.45 | 573... | 110.59 | 610... | 117.73 |
| 96.50 | 537... | 103.64 | 574... | 110.78 | 611... | 117.92 |
| 96.69 | 538... | 103.83 | 575... | 110.98 | 612... | 118.12 |
| 96.39 | 539... | 104.03 | 576... | 111.17 | 613... | 118.31 |
| 97.08 | 540... | 104.22 | 577... | 111.36 | 614... | 118.50 |
| 97.27 | 541... | 104.41 | 578... | 111.55 | 615... | 118.70 |
| 97.47 | 542... | 104.61 | 579... | 111.75 | 616... | 118.89 |
| 97.66 | 543... | 104.80 | 580... | 111.94 | 617... | 119.08 |
| 97.85 | 544... | 104.99 | 581... | 112.13 | 618... | 119.27 |
| 98.04 | 545... | 105.19 | 582... | 112.33 | 619... | 119.47 |
| 98.24 | 546... | 105.38 | 583... | 112.52 | 620... | 119.66 |
| 98.43 | 547... | 105.57 | 584... | 112.71 | 621... | 119.85 |
| 98.62 | 548... | 105.76 | 585... | 112.91 | 622... | 120.05 |
| 98.82 | 549... | 105.96 | 586... | 113.10 | 623... | 120.24 |
| 99.01 | 550... | 106.15 | 587... | 113.29 | 624... | 120.43 |
| 99.20 | 551... | 106.34 | 588... | 113.48 | 625... | 120.63 |
| 99.40 | 552... | 106.54 | 589... | 113.68 | 626... | 120.82 |
| 99.59 | 553... | 106.73 | 590... | 113.87 | 627... | 121.01 |

| F. | $ c. | F. | $ c. | F. | $ c. |
|---|---|---|---|---|---|
| 628 | 121.20 | 665 | 128.35 | 702 | 135.49 |
| 629 | 121.40 | 666 | 128.54 | 703 | 135.68 |
| 630 | 121.59 | 667 | 128.73 | 704 | 135.87 |
| 631 | 121.78 | 668 | 128.92 | 705 | 136.07 |
| 632 | 121.98 | 669 | 129.12 | 706 | 136.26 |
| 633 | 122.17 | 670 | 129.31 | 707 | 136.45 |
| 634 | 122.36 | 671 | 129.50 | 708 | 136.64 |
| 635 | 122.56 | 672 | 129.70 | 709 | 136.84 |
| 636 | 122.75 | 673 | 129.89 | 710 | 137.03 |
| 637 | 122.94 | 674 | 130.08 | 711 | 137.22 |
| 638 | 123.13 | 675 | 130.28 | 712 | 137.42 |
| 639 | 123.33 | 676 | 130.47 | 713 | 137.61 |
| 640 | 123.52 | 677 | 130.66 | 714 | 137.80 |
| 641 | 123.71 | 678 | 130.85 | 715 | 138.00 |
| 642 | 123.91 | 679 | 131.05 | 716 | 138.19 |
| 643 | 124.10 | 680 | 131.24 | 717 | 138.38 |
| 644 | 124.29 | 681 | 131.43 | 718 | 138.57 |
| 645 | 124.49 | 682 | 131.63 | 719 | 138.77 |
| 646 | 124.68 | 683 | 131.82 | 720 | 138.96 |
| 647 | 124.87 | 684 | 132.01 | 721 | 139.15 |
| 648 | 125.06 | 685 | 132.21 | 722 | 139.35 |
| 649 | 125.26 | 686 | 132.40 | 723 | 139.54 |
| 650 | 125.45 | 687 | 132.59 | 724 | 139.73 |
| 651 | 125.64 | 688 | 132.78 | 725 | 139.93 |
| 652 | 125.84 | 689 | 132.98 | 726 | 140.12 |
| 653 | 126.03 | 690 | 133.17 | 727 | 140.31 |
| 654 | 126.22 | 691 | 133.36 | 728 | 140.50 |
| 655 | 126.42 | 692 | 133.56 | 729 | 140.70 |
| 656 | 126.61 | 693 | 133.75 | 730 | 140.89 |
| 657 | 126.80 | 694 | 133.94 | 731 | 141.08 |
| 658 | 126.99 | 695 | 134.14 | 732 | 141.28 |
| 659 | 127.19 | 696 | 134.33 | 733 | 141.47 |
| 660 | 127.38 | 697 | 134.52 | 734 | 141.66 |
| 661 | 127.57 | 698 | 134.71 | 735 | 141.86 |
| 662 | 127.77 | 699 | 134.91 | 736 | 142.05 |
| 663 | 127.96 | 700 | 135.10 | 737 | 142.24 |
| 664 | 128.15 | 701 | 135.29 | 738 | 142.43 |

| F. | $ c. | F. | $ c. | F. | $ c. |
|---|---|---|---|---|---|
| 739... | 142.63 | 776... | 149.77 | 813... | 156.91 |
| 740... | 142.82 | 777... | 149.96 | 814... | 157.10 |
| 741... | 143.01 | 778... | 150.15 | 815... | 157.30 |
| 742... | 143.01 | 779... | 150.2 | 816... | 157.49 |
| 743... | 143.0 | 780... | 150.54 | 817... | 157.68 |
| 744... | 143.59 | 781... | 150.73 | 818... | 157.87 |
| 745... | 143.79 | 782.. | 150.93 | 819... | 158.07 |
| 746... | 143.98 | 783... | 151.12 | 820... | 158.26 |
| 747... | 144.17 | 784... | 151.31 | 821... | 158.45 |
| 748... | 144.36 | 785... | 151.51 | 822... | 158.65 |
| 749... | 144.56 | 786... | 151.70 | 823... | 158.84 |
| 750... | 144.75 | 787... | 151.89 | 824... | 159.03 |
| 751... | 144.94 | 788... | 152.08 | 825... | 159.23 |
| 752... | 145.14 | 789... | 152.28 | 826... | 159.42 |
| 753... | 145.33 | 790... | 152.47 | 827... | 159.61 |
| 754... | 145.52 | 791... | 152.66 | 828... | 159.80 |
| 755... | 145.72 | 792... | 152.86 | 829... | 160.00 |
| 756... | 145.91 | 793... | 153.05 | 830... | 160.19 |
| 757... | 146.10 | 794... | 153.24 | 831... | 160.38 |
| 758... | 146.29 | 795... | 153.44 | 832... | 160.58 |
| 759... | 146.49 | 796... | 153.63 | 833... | 160.77 |
| 760... | 146.68 | 797... | 153.82 | 834... | 160.96 |
| 761... | 146.87 | 798... | 154.01 | 835... | 161.16 |
| 762... | 147.07 | 799... | 154.21 | 836... | 161.35 |
| 763... | 147.26 | 800... | 154.40 | 837... | 161.54 |
| 764... | 147.45 | 801... | 154.59 | 838... | 161.73 |
| 765... | 147.65 | 802... | 154.79 | 839... | 161.93 |
| 766... | 147.84 | 803... | 154.98 | 840... | 162.12 |
| 767... | 148.03 | 804... | 155.17 | 841... | 162.31 |
| 768... | 148.22 | 805... | 155.37 | 842... | 162.51 |
| 769... | 148.42 | 806... | 155.56 | 843... | 162.70 |
| 770... | 148.61 | 807... | 155.75 | 844... | 162.89 |
| 771... | 148.80 | 808... | 155.94 | 845... | 163.09 |
| 772... | 149.00 | 809... | 156.14 | 846... | 163.28 |
| 773... | 149.19 | 810... | 156.33 | 847... | 163.47 |
| 774... | 149.38 | 811... | 156.52 | 848... | 163.66 |
| 775... | 149.58 | 812... | 156.72 | 849... | 163.86 |

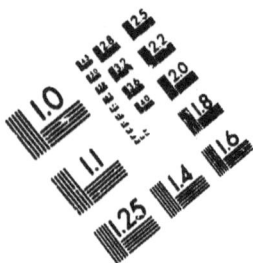

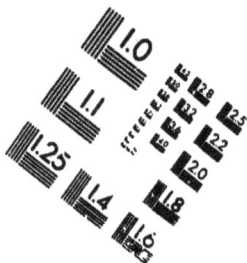

IMAGE EVALUATION
TEST TARGET (MT-3)

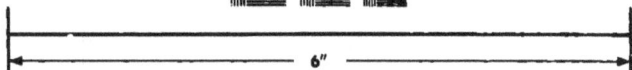

6"

Photographic
Sciences
Corporation

23 WEST MAIN STREET
WEBSTER, N.Y. 14580
(716) 872-4503

| F. | $ C. | F. | $ C. | F. | $ C. |
|---|---|---|---|---|---|
| 850... | 164.05 | 887... | 171.19 | 924... | 178.33 |
| 851... | 164.24 | 888... | 171.38 | 925... | 178.53 |
| 852... | 164.44 | 889... | 171.58 | 926... | 178.72 |
| 853... | 164.63 | 890... | 171.77 | 927... | 178.91 |
| 854... | 164.82 | 891... | 171.96 | 928... | 179.10 |
| 855... | 165.02 | 892... | 172.16 | 929... | 179.30 |
| 856... | 165.21 | 893... | 172.35 | 930... | 179.49 |
| 857... | 165.40 | 894... | 172.54 | 931... | 179.68 |
| 858... | 165.59 | 895... | 172.74 | 932... | 179.88 |
| 859... | 165.79 | 896... | 172.93 | 933... | 180.07 |
| 860... | 165.98 | 897... | 173.12 | 934... | 180.26 |
| 861... | 166.17 | 898... | 173.31 | 935... | 180.46 |
| 862... | 166.37 | 899... | 173.51 | 936... | 180.65 |
| 863... | 166.56 | 900... | 173.70 | 937... | 180.84 |
| 864... | 166.75 | 901... | 173.89 | 938... | 181.03 |
| 865... | 166.95 | 902... | 174.09 | 939... | 181.23 |
| 866... | 167.14 | 903... | 174.28 | 940... | 181.42 |
| 867... | 167.33 | 904... | 174.47 | 941... | 181.61 |
| 868... | 167.52 | 905... | 174.67 | 942... | 181.81 |
| 869... | 167.72 | 906... | 174.86 | 943... | 182.00 |
| 870... | 167.91 | 907... | 175.05 | 944... | 182.19 |
| 871... | 168.10 | 908... | 175 24 | 945... | 182.39 |
| 872... | 168.30 | 909... | 175.44 | 946... | 182.58 |
| 873... | 168.49 | 910... | 175.63 | 947... | 182.77 |
| 874... | 168.68 | 911... | 175.82 | 948... | 182.96 |
| 875... | 168.88 | 912... | 176.02 | 949... | 183.16 |
| 876... | 169.07 | 913... | 176.21 | 950... | 183.35 |
| 877... | 169.26 | 914... | 176.40 | 951... | 183.54 |
| 878... | 169.45 | 915... | 176.60 | 952... | 183.74 |
| 879... | 169.65 | 916... | 176.79 | 953... | 183.93 |
| 880... | 169.84 | 917... | 176.98 | 954... | 184.12 |
| 881... | 170.03 | 918... | 177.17 | 955... | 184.32 |
| 882... | 170.23 | 919... | 177.37 | 956... | 184.51 |
| 883... | 170.42 | 920... | 177.56 | 957... | 184.70 |
| 884... | 170.61 | 921... | 177.75 | 958... | 184.89 |
| 885... | 170.81 | 922... | 177.95 | 959... | 185.09 |
| 886... | 171.00 | 923... | 178.14 | 960... | 185.28 |

| F. | $ C. | F. | $ C. | F. | $ C. |
|---|---|---|---|---|---|
| 961... | 185.47 | 983... | 189.72 | 1500... | 289.50 |
| 962... | 185.67 | 984... | 189.91 | 1600... | 308.80 |
| 963... | 185.86 | 985... | 190.11 | 1700... | 328.10 |
| 964... | 186.05 | 986... | 190.30 | 1800... | 347.40 |
| 965... | 186.25 | 987... | 190.49 | 1900... | 366.70 |
| 966... | 186.44 | 988... | 190.68 | 2000... | 386.00 |
| 967... | 186.63 | 989... | 190.88 | 2500... | 482.50 |
| 968... | 186.82 | 990... | 191.07 | 3000... | 579.00 |
| 969... | 187.02 | 991... | 191.26 | 3500... | 675.50 |
| 970... | 187.21 | 992... | 191.46 | 4000... | 772.00 |
| 971... | 187.40 | 993... | 191.65 | 4500... | 868.50 |
| 972... | 187.60 | 994... | 191.84 | 5000... | 965.00 |
| 973... | 187.79 | 995... | 192.04 | 5500... | 1061.50 |
| 974... | 187.98 | 996... | 192.23 | 6000... | 1158.00 |
| 975... | 188.18 | 997... | 192.42 | 6500... | 1254.00 |
| 976... | 188.37 | 998... | 192.61 | 7000... | 1351.00 |
| 977... | 188.56 | 999... | 192.81 | 7500... | 1447.50 |
| 978... | 188.75 | 1000... | 193.00 | 8000... | 1544.00 |
| 979... | 188.95 | 1100... | 212.30 | 8500... | 1640.50 |
| 980... | 189.14 | 1200... | 231.60 | 9000... | 1737.00 |
| 981... | 189.33 | 1300... | 250.90 | 9500... | 1833.50 |
| 982... | 189.53 | 1400... | 270.20 | 10000... | 1920.00 |

# GERMAN RIXMARK

### REDUCED TO

## DOLLARS AND CENTS

### At the Customs Value of 23.8 Cents.

| RM. | $ c. | RM. | $ c. | RM. | $ c. |
|---|---|---|---|---|---|
| 1... | .24 | 26... | 6.19 | 51... | 12.14 |
| 2... | .48 | 27... | 6.43 | 52... | 12.38 |
| 3... | .71 | 28... | 6.66 | 53... | 12.61 |
| 4... | .95 | 29... | 6.90 | 54... | 12.85 |
| 5... | 1.19 | 30... | 7.14 | 55... | 13.09 |
| 6... | 1.43 | 31... | 7.38 | 56... | 13.33 |
| 7... | 1.67 | 32... | 7.62 | 57... | 13.57 |
| 8... | 1.90 | 33... | 7.85 | 58... | 13.80 |
| 9... | 2.14 | 34... | 8.09 | 59... | 14.04 |
| 10... | 2.38 | 35... | 8.33 | 60... | 14.28 |
| 11... | 2.62 | 36... | 8.57 | 61... | 14.52 |
| 12... | 2.86 | 37... | 8.81 | 62... | 14.76 |
| 13... | 3.09 | 38... | 9.04 | 63... | 14.99 |
| 14... | 3.33 | 39... | 9.28 | 64... | 15.23 |
| 15... | 3.57 | 40... | 9.52 | 65... | 15.47 |
| 16 .. | 3.81 | 41... | 9.76 | 66... | 15.71 |
| 17... | 4.05 | 42... | 10.00 | 67... | 15.95 |
| 18... | 4.28 | 43... | 10.23 | 68... | 16.18 |
| 19... | 4.52 | 44... | 10.47 | 69... | 16.42 |
| 20... | 4.76 | 45... | 10.71 | 70... | 16.66 |
| 21... | 5.00 | 46... | 10.95 | 71... | 16.90 |
| 22... | 5.24 | 47... | 11.19 | 72... | 17.14 |
| 23... | 5.47 | 48... | 11.42 | 73... | 17.37 |
| 24... | 5.71 | 49... | 11.66 | 74... | 17.61 |
| 25... | 5.95 | 50... | 11.90 | 75... | 17.85 |

ARK

ENTS

Cents.

| $ c. |
|------|
| 12.14 |
| 12.38 |
| 12.61 |
| 12.85 |
| 13.09 |
| 13.33 |
| 13.57 |
| 13.80 |
| 14.04 |
| 14.28 |
| 14.52 |
| 14.76 |
| 14.99 |
| 15.23 |
| 15.47 |
| 15.71 |
| 15.95 |
| 16.18 |
| 16.42 |
| 16.66 |
| 16.90 |
| 17.14 |
| 17.37 |
| 17.61 |
| 17.85 |

| RM. | $ c. | RM. | $ c. | RM. | $ c. |
|-----|------|-----|------|-----|------|
| 76... | 18.09 | 113... | 26 89 | 150... | 35.70 |
| 77... | 18.33 | 114... | 27.13 | 151... | 35.94 |
| 78... | 18.56 | 115... | 27.37 | 152... | 36.18 |
| 79... | 18.80 | 116... | 27.61 | 153... | 36.41 |
| 80... | 19.04 | 117... | 27.85 | 154... | 36.65 |
| 81... | 19.28 | 118... | 28.08 | 155... | 36.89 |
| 82... | 19.52 | 119... | 28.32 | 156... | 37.13 |
| 83... | 19.75 | 120... | 28.56 | 157... | 37.37 |
| 84... | 19.99 | 121... | 28.80 | 158... | 37.60 |
| 85.. | 20.23 | 122... | 29.04 | 159... | 37.84 |
| 86... | 20.47 | 123... | 29.27 | 160... | 38.08 |
| 87.. | 20.71 | 124... | 29.51 | 161... | 38.32 |
| 88... | 20.94 | 125... | 29.75 | 162... | 38.56 |
| 89... | 21.18 | 126... | 29.99 | 163... | 38.79 |
| 90 .. | 21.42 | 127... | 30.23 | 164... | 39.03 |
| 91... | 21.66 | 128... | 30.46 | 165... | 39.27 |
| 92... | 21.90 | 129... | 30.70 | 166... | 39.51 |
| 93... | 22.13 | 130... | 30.94 | 167... | 39.75 |
| 94... | 22.37 | 131... | 31.18 | 168... | 39.98 |
| 95... | 22.61 | 132... | 31.42 | 169... | 40.22 |
| 96... | 22.85 | 133... | 31.65 | 170... | 40.46 |
| 97... | 23.09 | 134... | 31.89 | 171... | 40.70 |
| 98... | 23.32 | 135... | 32.13 | 172... | 40.94 |
| 99.. | 23.56 | 136... | 32.37 | 173... | 41.17 |
| 100... | 23.80 | 137... | 32.61 | 174... | 41.41 |
| 101... | 24.04 | 138... | 32.84 | 175... | 41.65 |
| 102... | 24.28 | 139... | 33.08 | 176... | 41.89 |
| 103... | 24.51 | 140... | 33.32 | 177... | 42.13 |
| 104... | 24.75 | 141... | 33.56 | 178... | 42.36 |
| 105... | 24.99 | 142... | 33.80 | 179... | 42.60 |
| 106... | 25.23 | 143... | 34.03 | 180... | 42.84 |
| 107... | 25.47 | 144... | 34.27 | 181... | 43.08 |
| 108... | 25.70 | 145... | 34.51 | 182... | 43.32 |
| 109 .. | 25.94 | 146... | 34.75 | 183... | 43.55 |
| 110... | 26.18 | 147... | 34.99 | 184... | 43.79 |
| 111... | 26.42 | 148... | 35.22 | 185... | 44.03 |
| 112 .. | 26.66 | 149... | 35.46 | 186... | 44.27 |

| RM. | $ c. | RM. | $ c. | RM. | $ c. |
|---|---|---|---|---|---|
| 187... | 44.51 | 224... | 53.31 | 261... | 62.12 |
| 188... | 44.74 | 225... | 53.55 | 262... | 62.36 |
| 189... | 44.98 | 226... | 53.79 | 263... | 62.53 |
| 190... | 45.22 | 227... | 54.03 | 264... | 62.83 |
| 191... | 45.46 | 228... | 54.26 | 265... | 63.07 |
| 192... | 45.70 | 229... | 54.50 | 266... | 63.31 |
| 193... | 45.93 | 230... | 54.74 | 267... | 63.55 |
| 194... | 46.17 | 231... | 54.98 | 268... | 63.78 |
| 195... | 46.41 | 232... | 55.22 | 269... | 64.02 |
| 196... | 46.65 | 233... | 55.45 | 270... | 64.26 |
| 197... | 46.89 | 234... | 55.69 | 271... | 64.50 |
| 198... | 47.12 | 235... | 55.93 | 272... | 64.74 |
| 199... | 47.36 | 236... | 56.17 | 273... | 64.97 |
| 200... | 47.60 | 237... | 56.41 | 274... | 65.21 |
| 201... | 47.84 | 238... | 56.64 | 275... | 65.45 |
| 202... | 48.08 | 239 .. | 56.88 | 276... | 65.69 |
| 203... | 48.31 | 240... | 57.12 | 277... | 65.93 |
| 204... | 48.55 | 241... | 57.36 | 278... | 66.16 |
| 205... | 48.79 | 242... | 57.60 | 279... | 66.40 |
| 206... | 49.03 | 243... | 57.83 | 280... | 66.64 |
| 207... | 49.27 | 244... | 58.07 | 281... | 66.88 |
| 208... | 49.50 | 245... | 58.31 | 282... | 67.12 |
| 209... | 49.74 | 246... | 58.55 | 283... | 67.35 |
| 210... | 49.98 | 247... | 58.79 | 284... | 67.59 |
| 211... | 50 22 | 248... | 59.02 | 285... | 67.83 |
| 212... | 50.46 | 249... | 59.26 | 286... | 68.07 |
| 213... | 50.69 | 250... | 59.50 | 287... | 68:31 |
| 214... | 50.93 | 251... | 59.74 | 288... | 68.54 |
| 215... | 51.17 | 252... | 59.98 | 289... | 68.78 |
| 216... | 51.41 | 253... | 60.21 | 290... | 69.02 |
| 217... | 51.65 | 254... | 60.45 | 291... | 69.26 |
| 218.. | 51.88 | 255... | 60.69 | 292... | 69.50 |
| 219... | 52.12 | 256... | 60.93 | 293... | 69.73 |
| 220... | 52.36 | 257... | 61.17 | 294... | 69.97 |
| 221.. | 52.60 | 258... | 61.40 | 295... | 70.21 |
| 222... | 52.84 | 259... | 61.64 | 296... | 70.45 |
| 223... | 53.07 | 260... | 61.88 | 297... | 70.69 |

| R.M. | $ c. | R.M. | $ c. | R.M. | $ c. |
|------|------|------|------|------|------|
| 298... | 70.92 | 335 .. | 79.73 | 372... | 88.54 |
| 299... | 71.16 | 336... | 79.97 | 373... | 88.77 |
| 300... | 71.40 | 337... | 80.21 | 374... | 89.01 |
| 301... | 71.64 | 338... | 80.44 | 375... | 89.25 |
| 302... | 71.88 | 339... | 80.68 | 376... | 89.49 |
| 303... | 72.11 | 340... | 80.92 | 377... | 89.73 |
| 304... | 72.35 | 341... | 81.16 | 378... | 89.96 |
| 305... | 72.59 | 342... | 81.40 | 379... | 90.20 |
| 306... | 72.83 | 343... | 81.63 | 380... | 90.44 |
| 307... | 73.07 | 344... | 81.87 | 381... | 90.68 |
| 308... | 73.30 | 345... | 82.11 | 382... | 90.92 |
| 309... | 73.54 | 346... | 82.35 | 383... | 91.15 |
| 310... | 73.78 | 347... | 82.59 | 384... | 91.39 |
| 311... | 74.02 | 348... | 82.82 | 385... | 91.63 |
| 312... | 74.26 | 349... | 83.06 | 386... | 91.87 |
| 313... | 74.49 | 350... | 83.30 | 387... | 92.11 |
| 314... | 74.73 | 351... | 83.54 | 388... | 92.34 |
| 315... | 74.97 | 352... | 83.78 | 389... | 92.58 |
| 316... | 75.21 | 353... | 84.01 | 390... | 92.82 |
| 317... | 75.45 | 354... | 84.25 | 391... | 93.06 |
| 318... | 75.68 | 355... | 84.49 | 392... | 93.30 |
| 319... | 75.92 | 356... | 84.73 | 393... | 93.53 |
| 320... | 76.16 | 357... | 84.97 | 394... | 93.77 |
| 321... | 76.40 | 358... | 85.20 | 395 .. | 94.01 |
| 322... | 76.64 | 359... | 85.44 | 396... | 94.25 |
| 323... | 76.87 | 360... | 85.68 | 397... | 94.49 |
| 324... | 77.11 | 361... | 85.92 | 398... | 94.72 |
| 325... | 77.35 | 362... | 86.16 | 399... | 94.96 |
| 326... | 77.59 | 363... | 86.39 | 400... | 95.20 |
| 327... | 77.83 | 364... | 86.63 | 401... | 95.44 |
| 328... | 78.06 | 365... | 86.87 | 402... | 95.68 |
| 329... | 78.30 | 366... | 87.11 | 403... | 95.91 |
| 330... | 78.54 | 367... | 87.35 | 404... | 96.15 |
| 331... | 78.78 | 368... | 87.58 | 405... | 96.39 |
| 332... | 79.02 | 369... | 87.82 | 406... | 96.63 |
| 333... | 79.25 | 370... | 88.06 | 407... | 96.87 |
| 334... | 79.49 | 371... | 88.30 | 408... | 97.10 |

| RE. | $ c. | RM. | $ c. | RM. | $ c |
|---|---|---|---|---|---|
| 409... | 97.34 | 446... | 106.15 | 483... | 114.95 |
| 410... | 97.58 | 447... | 106.39 | 484... | 115.19 |
| 411... | 97.82 | 448... | 106.62 | 485... | 115.43 |
| 412... | 98.06 | 449... | 106.86 | 486... | 115.67 |
| 413... | 98.29 | 450... | 107.10 | 487... | 115.91 |
| 414... | 98.53 | 451... | 107.34 | 488... | 116.14 |
| 415... | 98.77 | 452... | 107.58 | 489... | 116.38 |
| 416... | 99.01 | 453... | 107.81 | 490... | 116.62 |
| 417... | 99.25 | 454... | 108.05 | 491... | 116.86 |
| 418... | 99.48 | 455... | 108.29 | 492... | 117.10 |
| 419... | 99.72 | 456... | 108.53 | 493... | 117.33 |
| 420... | 99.96 | 457... | 108.77 | 494... | 117.57 |
| 421... | 100.20 | 458... | 109.00 | 495... | 117.81 |
| 422... | 100.44 | 459... | 109.24 | 496... | 118.05 |
| 423... | 100.67 | 460... | 109.48 | 497... | 118.29 |
| 424... | 100.91 | 461.. | 109.72 | 498... | 118.52 |
| 425... | 101.15 | 462... | 109.96 | 499... | 118.76 |
| 426... | 101.39 | 463... | 110.19 | 500... | 119.00 |
| 427... | 101.63 | 464... | 110.43 | 501... | 119.24 |
| 428 .. | 101.86 | 465... | 110.67 | 502... | 119.48 |
| 429... | 102.10 | 466... | 110.91 | 503... | 119.71 |
| 430... | 102.34 | 467... | 111.15 | 504... | 119.95 |
| 431... | 102.58 | 468... | 111.38 | 505... | 120.19 |
| 432... | 102.82 | 469... | 111.62 | 506... | 120.43 |
| 433... | 103.05 | 470... | 111.86 | 507... | 120.67 |
| 434... | 103.29 | 471... | 112.10 | 508... | 120.90 |
| 435... | 103.53 | 472... | 112.34 | 509... | 121.14 |
| 436 . | 103.77 | 473... | 112.57 | 510... | 121.38 |
| 437... | 104 01 | 474... | 112.81 | 511... | 121.62 |
| 438... | 104.24 | 475... | 113.05 | 512... | 121.86 |
| 439... | 104.48 | 476... | 113.29 | 513... | 122.09 |
| 440... | 104.72 | 477... | 113.53 | 514... | 122.33 |
| 441... | 104.96 | 478.. | 113.76 | 515... | 122.57 |
| 442... | 105.20 | 479... | 114.00 | 516... | 122.81 |
| 443... | 105.43 | 480... | 114.24 | 517... | 123.05 |
| 444... | 105.67 | 481... | 114.48 | 518... | 123.28 |
| 445... | 105.91 | 482... | 114.72 | 519... | 123.52 |

| RM. | $ C. | RM. | $ C. | RM. | $ C. |
|---|---|---|---|---|---|
| 520... | 123.76 | 557... | 132.57 | 594... | 141.37 |
| 521... | 124.00 | 558... | 132.80 | 595... | 141.61 |
| 522... | 124.24 | 559... | 133.04 | 596... | 141.85 |
| 523... | 124.47 | 560... | 133.28 | 597... | 142.09 |
| 524... | 124.71 | 561... | 133.52 | 598... | 142.32 |
| 525... | 124.95 | 562... | 133.76 | 599... | 142.56 |
| 526... | 125.19 | 563... | 133.99 | 600... | 142.80 |
| 527... | 125.43 | 564... | 134.23 | 601... | 143.04 |
| 528... | 125.66 | 565... | 134.47 | 602... | 143.28 |
| 529... | 125.90 | 566... | 134.71 | 603... | 143.51 |
| 530... | 126.14 | 567... | 134.95 | 604... | 143.75 |
| 531... | 126.38 | 568... | 135.18 | 605... | 143.99 |
| 532... | 126.62 | 569... | 135.42 | 606... | 144.23 |
| 533... | 126.85 | 570... | 135.66 | 607... | 144.47 |
| 534... | 127.09 | 571... | 135.90 | 608... | 144.70 |
| 535... | 127.33 | 572... | 136.14 | 609... | 144.94 |
| 536... | 127.57 | 573... | 136.37 | 610... | 145.18 |
| 537... | 127.81 | 574... | 136.61 | 611... | 145.42 |
| 538... | 128.04 | 575... | 136.85 | 612... | 145.66 |
| 539... | 128.28 | 576... | 137.09 | 613... | 145.89 |
| 540... | 128.52 | 577... | 137.33 | 614... | 146.13 |
| 541... | 128.76 | 578... | 137.56 | 615... | 146.37 |
| 542... | 129.00 | 579... | 137.80 | 616... | 146.61 |
| 543... | 129.23 | 580... | 138.04 | 617... | 146.85 |
| 544 .. | 129.47 | 581... | 138.28 | 618... | 147.08 |
| 545... | 129.71 | 582... | 138.52 | 619... | 147.32 |
| 546... | 129.95 | 583... | 138.75 | 620... | 147.56 |
| 547... | 130.19 | 584... | 138.99 | 621... | 147.80 |
| 548... | 130.42 | 585... | 139.23 | 622... | 148.04 |
| 549... | 130.66 | 586... | 139.47 | 623... | 148.27 |
| 550... | 130.90 | 587... | 139.71 | 624... | 148.51 |
| 551... | 131.14 | 588... | 139.94 | 625... | 148.75 |
| 552... | 131.38 | 589... | 140.18 | 626... | 148.99 |
| 553... | 131.61 | 590... | 140.42 | 627... | 149.23 |
| 554... | 131.85 | 591... | 140.66 | 628... | 149.46 |
| 555... | 132.09 | 592... | 140.90 | 629... | 149.70 |
| 556... | 132.33 | 593... | 141.13 | 630... | 149.94 |

G

| RM. | $ C. | RM. | $ C. | RM. | $ C. |
|---|---|---|---|---|---|
| 631... | 150.18 | 668... | 158.98 | 705... | 167.79 |
| 632... | 150.42 | 669... | 159.22 | 706... | 168.03 |
| 633... | 150.65 | 670... | 159.46 | 707... | 168.27 |
| 634... | 150.89 | 671... | 159.70 | 708... | 168.50 |
| 635... | 151.13 | 672... | 159.94 | 709... | 168.74 |
| 636... | 151.37 | 673... | 160.17 | 710... | 168.98 |
| 637... | 151.61 | 674... | 160.41 | 711... | 169.22 |
| 638... | 151.84 | 675... | 160.65 | 712... | 169.46 |
| 639... | 152.08 | 676... | 160.89 | 713... | 169.69 |
| 640... | 152.32 | 677... | 161.13 | 714... | 169.93 |
| 641... | 152.56 | 678... | 161.36 | 715... | 170.17 |
| 642... | 152.80 | 679... | 161.60 | 716... | 170.41 |
| 643... | 153.03 | 680... | 161.84 | 717... | 170.65 |
| 644... | 153.27 | 681... | 162.08 | 718... | 170.88 |
| 645... | 153.51 | 682... | 162.32 | 719... | 171.12 |
| 646... | 153.75 | 683... | 162.55 | 720... | 171.36 |
| 647... | 153.99 | 684... | 162.79 | 721... | 171.60 |
| 648... | 154.22 | 685... | 163.03 | 722... | 171.84 |
| 649... | 154.46 | 686... | 163.27 | 723... | 172.07 |
| 650... | 154.70 | 687... | 163.51 | 724... | 172.31 |
| 651... | 154.94 | 688... | 163.74 | 725... | 172.55 |
| 652... | 155.18 | 689... | 163.98 | 726... | 172.79 |
| 653... | 155.41 | 690... | 164.22 | 727... | 173.03 |
| 654... | 155.65 | 691... | 164.46 | 728... | 173.26 |
| 655... | 155.89 | 692... | 164.70 | 729... | 173.50 |
| 656... | 156.13 | 693... | 164.93 | 730... | 173.74 |
| 657... | 156.37 | 694... | 165.17 | 731... | 173.98 |
| 658... | 156.60 | 695... | 165.41 | 732... | 174.22 |
| 659... | 156.84 | 696... | 165.65 | 733... | 174.45 |
| 660... | 157.08 | 697... | 165.89 | 734... | 174.69 |
| 661... | 157.32 | 698... | 166.12 | 735... | 174.93 |
| 662... | 157.56 | 699... | 166.36 | 736... | 175.17 |
| 663... | 157.79 | 700... | 166.60 | 737... | 175.41 |
| 664... | 158.03 | 701... | 166.84 | 738... | 175.64 |
| 665... | 158.27 | 702... | 167.08 | 739... | 175.88 |
| 666... | 158.51 | 703... | 167.31 | 740... | 176.12 |
| 667... | 158.75 | 704... | 167.55 | 741... | 176.36 |

| RM. | $ C. | RM. | $ C. | RM. | $ C. |
|---|---|---|---|---|---|
| 742... | 176.60 | 779... | 185.40 | 816... | 194.21 |
| 743... | 176.83 | 780... | 185.64 | 817... | 194.45 |
| 744... | 177.07 | 781... | 185.88 | 818... | 194.68 |
| 745... | 177.31 | 782... | 186.12 | 819... | 194.92 |
| 746... | 177.55 | 783... | 186.35 | 820... | 195.16 |
| 747... | 177.79 | 784... | 186.59 | 821... | 195.40 |
| 748... | 178.02 | 785... | 186.83 | 822... | 195.64 |
| 749... | 178.26 | 786... | 187.07 | 823... | 195.87 |
| 750... | 178.50 | 787... | 187.31 | 824... | 196.11 |
| 751... | 178.74 | 788... | 187.54 | 825... | 196.35 |
| 752... | 178.98 | 789... | 187.78 | 826... | 196.59 |
| 753... | 179.21 | 790... | 188.02 | 827 .. | 196.83 |
| 754.. | 179.45 | 791... | 188.26 | 828... | 197.06 |
| 755... | 179.69 | 792 .. | 188.50 | 829... | 197.30 |
| 756... | 179.93 | 793... | 188.73 | 830... | 197.54 |
| 757... | 180.17 | 794... | 188.97 | 831... | 197.78 |
| 758... | 180.40 | 795... | 189.21 | 832... | 198.02 |
| 759... | 180.64 | 796.. | 189.45 | 833... | 198.25 |
| 760... | 180.88 | 797... | 189.69 | 834... | 198.49 |
| 761... | 181.12 | 798... | 189.92 | 835... | 198.73 |
| 762... | 181.36 | 799... | 190.16 | 836... | 198.97 |
| 763... | 181.59 | 800... | 190.40 | 837... | 199.21 |
| 764... | 181.83 | 801... | 190.64 | 838... | 199.44 |
| 765... | 182.07 | 802... | 190.88 | 839... | 199.68 |
| 766... | 182.31 | 803... | 191.11 | 840... | 199.92 |
| 767... | 182.55 | 804... | 191.35 | 841... | 200.16 |
| 768... | 182.78 | 805... | 191.59 | 842... | 200.40 |
| 769... | 183.02 | 806... | 191.83 | 843... | 200.63 |
| 770... | 183.26 | 807... | 192.07 | 844... | 200.87 |
| 771... | 183.50 | 808... | 192.30 | 845... | 201.11 |
| 772... | 183.74 | 809... | 192.54 | 846... | 201.35 |
| 773... | 183.97 | 810... | 192.78 | 847... | 201.59 |
| 774... | 184.21 | 811... | 193.02 | 848... | 201.82 |
| 775... | 184.45 | 812... | 193.26 | 849... | 202.06 |
| 776... | 184.69 | 813... | 193.49 | 850... | 202.30 |
| 777... | 184.93 | 814... | 193.73 | 851... | 202.54 |
| 778... | 185.16 | 815... | 193.97 | 852... | 202.78 |

| RM. | $ C. | RM. | $ C. | RM. | $ C. |
|---|---|---|---|---|---|
| 853... | 203.01 | 890... | 211.82 | 927... | 220.63 |
| 854... | 203.25 | 891... | 212.06 | 928... | 220.86 |
| 855... | 203.49 | 892... | 212.30 | 929... | 221.10 |
| 856... | 203.73 | 893... | 212.53 | 930... | 221.84 |
| 857... | 203.97 | 894... | 212.77 | 931... | 221.58 |
| 858... | 204.20 | 895... | 213.01 | 932... | 221.82 |
| 859... | 204.44 | 896... | 213.25 | 933... | 222.05 |
| 860... | 204.68 | 897... | 213.49 | 934... | 222.29 |
| 861... | 204.92 | 898... | 213.72 | 935... | 222.53 |
| 862... | 205.16 | 899... | 213.96 | 936.. | 222.77 |
| 863... | 205.39 | 900... | 214.20 | 937... | 223.01 |
| 864... | 205.63 | 901... | 214.44 | 938... | 223.24 |
| 865... | 205.87 | 902... | 214.68 | 939... | 223.48 |
| 866... | 206.11 | 903... | 214.91 | 940... | 223.72 |
| 867... | 206.35 | 904... | 215.15 | 941... | 223.96 |
| 868... | 206.58 | 905... | 215.39 | 942... | 224.20 |
| 869... | 206.82 | 906... | 215.63 | 943... | 224.43 |
| 870... | 207.06 | 907... | 215.87 | 944... | 224.67 |
| 871... | 207.30 | 908... | 216.10 | 945... | 224.91 |
| 872... | 207.54 | 909... | 216.34 | 946... | 225.15 |
| 873... | 207.77 | 910... | 216.58 | 947... | 225.39 |
| 874... | 208.01 | 911... | 216.82 | 948... | 225.62 |
| 875... | 208.25 | 912... | 217.06 | 949... | 225.86 |
| 876... | 208.49 | 913... | 217.29 | 950... | 226.10 |
| 877... | 208.73 | 914... | 217 53 | 951... | 226.34 |
| 878... | 208.96 | 915... | 217.77 | 952... | 226.58 |
| 879... | 209.20 | 916... | 218.01 | 953... | 226.81 |
| 880... | 209.44 | 917... | 218.25 | 954... | 227.05 |
| 881... | 209.68 | 918... | 218.48 | 955... | 227.29 |
| 882 .. | 209.92 | 919... | 218.72 | 956... | 227.53 |
| 883... | 210.15 | 920... | 218.96 | 957... | 227.77 |
| 884... | 210.39 | 921... | 219.20 | 958... | 228.00 |
| 885... | 210.63 | 922... | 219.44 | 959... | 228.24 |
| 886... | 210.87 | 923... | 219.67 | 960... | 228.48 |
| 887... | 211.11 | 924... | 219.91 | 961... | 228.72 |
| 888... | 211.34 | 925... | 220.15 | 962... | 228.96 |
| 889... | 211.58 | 926... | 220.39 | 963... | 229.19 |

| RM. | $ c. | RM. | $ c. | RM. | $ c. |
|---|---|---|---|---|---|
| 964... | 229.43 | 983... | 233.95 | 1100... | 261.80 |
| 965... | 229.67 | 984... | 234.19 | 1200... | 285.60 |
| 966... | 229.91 | 985... | 234.43 | 1300... | 309.40 |
| 967... | 230.15 | 986... | 234.67 | 1400... | 333.20 |
| 968... | 230.38 | 987... | 234.91 | 1500 .. | 357.00 |
| 969... | 230.62 | 988... | 235.14 | 1600... | 380.80 |
| 970 .. | 230.86 | 989... | 235.38 | 1700... | 404.60 |
| 971... | 231.10 | 990... | 235.62 | 1800... | 428.40 |
| 972... | 231.34 | 991... | 235.86 | 1900... | 452.20 |
| 973... | 231.57 | 992... | 236.10 | 2000... | 476.00 |
| 974... | 231.81 | 993... | 236.33 | 3000... | 714.00 |
| 975... | 232.05 | 994... | 236.57 | 4000... | 952.00 |
| 976... | 232.29 | 995... | 236.81 | 5000... | 1190.00 |
| 977... | 232.53 | 996... | 237.05 | 6000... | 1428.00 |
| 978... | 232.76 | 997... | 237.29 | 7000... | 1666.00 |
| 979... | 233.00 | 998... | 237.52 | 8000... | 1904.00 |
| 980... | 233.24 | 999... | 237.76 | 9000... | 2142.00 |
| 981... | 233.48 | 1000... | 238.00 | 10000... | 2380.00 |
| 982... | 233.72 | | | | |

Fractional Currency,=100 Pfennig equal to one Rixmark.

# TABLE

SHOWING THE

# CANADIAN CUSTOMS VALUES

OF THE

## PRINCIPAL FOREIGN CURRENCIES.

| COUNTRY | MONETARY UNIT. | STANDARD. | Value in Dollars and Cents. |
|---|---|---|---|
| Austria............... | .... Florin ........ | | |
| Belgium ............... | ........ Franc ........ | Gold & Silver | $0.19.3 |
| Bolivia ................ | ........ Dollar ........ | Gold & Silver | .96.5 |
| Brazil ................. | ... ....Milreis ......... | ..... Gold .... | .54.5 |
| Bogota.... ........... | ........ Peso ......... | ..... Gold ..... | .90.5 |
| Central America...... | ........ Dollar ........ | .... Silver .... | .93.5 |
| Chili..... ............. | ........ Peso ........ | ..... Gold ..... | .91.2 |
| China ............... | ........ Tael ........ | | |
| Denmark............. | ........ Crown ....... | ..... Gold ..... | .26.8 |
| Ecuador............. | ........ Dollar ...... | .... Silver .... | .93.5 |
| Egypt .............. | Pound of 100 piastres | ..... Gold .... | 4.97.4 |
| France .......... . | ........ Franc ....... | Gold & Silver | .19.3 |
| Greece.................. | ..... Drachma ...... | Gold & Silver | .19.3 |
| German Empire...... | ........ Mark .... .. | .... Gold .... | .23.8 |
| Japan ............... | ........ Yen ........ | .... Gold .... | .99.7 |
| India ................ | Rupee of 16 annas | .... Silver .... | .44.4 |
| Italy ............... | ........ Lira ........ | Gold & Silver | .19.3 |
| Liberia ............... | ........ Dollar ........ | ..... Gold ...... | 1.00. |
| Mexico ............. | ........ Dollar ........ | .. Silver .... | 1.01.5 |
| Netherlands ........... | ... ... Florin ........ | Gold & Silver | .38.5 |
| Norway............... | ........ Crown ........ | .... Gold . ... | .26.8 |
| Peru .. ............. | ........ Dollar ........ | .... Silver .. . | .93.5 |
| Portugal .... ...... | ........ Milreis ........ | .... Gold ..... | 1.08. |
| Russia .............. | ........ Rouble ... .... | .... Silver .... | .74.8 |
| Sandwich Islands .... | ........ Dollar ........ | .... Gold ..... | 1.00. |
| Spain .............. | Peseta of 100 centimes | Gold & Silver | .19 3 |
| Sweden ............. | ........ Crown ........ | .... Gold .... | .26.8 |
| Switzerland ........... | ........ Franc ........ | Gold & Silver | .19 3 |
| Tripoli ............... | Mahbub of 20 piastres | .... Silver .... | .84.4 |
| Turkey............... | ........ Piaster ........ | .... Gold ..... | .04.3 |
| United States of Colombia | ........ Peso ........ | .... Silver .... | .93.5 |

## THE VALUE OF FRANCS IN ENGLISH MONEY.

**Valeur des Francs en Monnaie Anglaise.**

| Fr. Cts. | | £ | s. | d. | Fr. Cts. | | £ | s. | d. |
|---|---|---|---|---|---|---|---|---|---|
| . 5 | = | .. | .. | ½ | 1 70 | = | .. | 1 | 4⅜ |
| . 10 | " | .. | .. | 1 | 1 75 | " | .. | 1 | 4¾ |
| . 15 | " | .. | .. | 1½ | 1 80 | " | .. | 1 | 5¼ |
| . 20 | " | .. | .. | 1⅞ | 1 90 | " | .. | 1 | 6¼ |
| . 25 | " | .. | .. | 2⅜ | 2 .. | " | .. | 1 | 7⅛ |
| . 30 | " | .. | .. | 2⅞ | 2 10 | " | .. | 1 | 8⅛ |
| . 35 | " | .. | .. | 3⅜ | 2 20 | " | .. | 1 | 9⅛ |
| . 40 | " | .. | .. | 3⅞ | 2 25 | " | .. | 1 | 9⅜ |
| . 45 | " | .. | .. | 4⅜ | 2 30 | " | .. | 1 | 10⅛ |
| . 50 | " | .. | .. | 4¾ | 2 40 | " | .. | 1 | 11 |
| . 55 | " | .. | .. | 5¼ | **2 50** | " | .. | **2** | .. |
| . 60 | " | .. | .. | 5¾ | 2 60 | " | .. | 2 | 1 |
| . 65 | " | .. | .. | 6¼ | 2 70 | " | .. | 2 | 1⅞ |
| . 70 | " | .. | .. | 6¾ | 2 75 | " | .. | 2 | 2⅜ |
| . 75 | " | .. | .. | 7¼ | 2 80 | " | .. | 2 | 2⅞ |
| . 80 | " | .. | .. | 7⅝ | 2 90 | " | .. | 2 | 3⅞ |
| . 85 | " | .. | .. | 8⅛ | 3 .. | " | .. | 2 | 4¾ |
| . 90 | " | .. | .. | 8⅝ | 3 10 | " | .. | 2 | 5¾ |
| . 95 | " | .. | .. | 9⅛ | 3 20 | " | .. | 2 | 6¾ |
| 1 .. | " | .. | .. | 9⅝ | 3 25 | " | .. | 2 | 7¼ |
| 1 10 | " | .. | .. | 10½ | 3 30 | " | .. | 2 | 7⅝ |
| 1 20 | " | .. | .. | 11½ | 3 40 | " | .. | 2 | 8⅜ |
| **1 25** | " | . | **1** | .. | 3 50 | " | .. | 2 | 9⅝ |
| 1 30 | " | .. | 1 | ½ | 3 60 | " | .. | 2 | 10½ |
| 1 40 | " | .. | 1 | 1½ | 3 70 | " | .. | 2 | 11½ |
| 1 50 | " | .. | 1 | 2⅜ | **3 75** | " | .. | **3** | .. |
| 1 60 | " | .. | 1 | 3⅜ | 3 80 | " | .. | 3 | ..½ |

| Fr. Cts. | | £ | s. | d. | Fr. Cts. | | £ | s. | d. |
|---|---|---|---|---|---|---|---|---|---|
| 3 90 | = | .. | 3 | 1½ | 6 40 | = | .. | 5 | 1½ |
| 4 .. | " | .. | 3 | 2⅜ | 6 50 | " | .. | 5 | 2⅜ |
| 4 10 | " | .. | 3 | 3⅜ | 6 60 | " | .. | 5 | 3⅜ |
| 4 20 | " | .. | 3 | 4⅜ | 6 70 | " | .. | 5 | 4⅜ |
| 4 25 | " | .. | 3 | 4¾ | 6 75 | " | .. | 5 | 4¾ |
| 4 30 | " | .. | 3 | 5¼ | 6 80 | " | .. | 5 | 5¼ |
| 4 40 | " | .. | 3 | 6¼ | 6 90 | " | .. | 5 | 6¼ |
| 4 50 | " | .. | 3 | 7⅛ | 7 .. | " | .. | 5 | 7⅛ |
| 4 60 | " | .. | 3 | 8⅛ | 7 10 | " | .. | 5 | 8⅛ |
| 4 70 | " | .. | 3 | 9⅛ | 7 20 | " | .. | 5 | 9⅛ |
| 4 75 | " | .. | 3 | 9⅝ | 7 25 | " | .. | 5 | 9⅝ |
| 4 80 | " | .. | 3 | 10⅛ | 7 30 | " | .. | 5 | 10⅛ |
| 4 90 | " | .. | 3 | 11 | 7 40 | " | .. | 5 | 11 |
| **5 ..** | " | .. | **4** | .. | **7 50** | " | .. | **6** | .. |
| 5 10 | " | .. | 4 | 1 | 7 60 | " | .. | 6 | 1 |
| 5 20 | " | .. | 4 | 1⅞ | 7 70 | " | .. | 6 | 1⅞ |
| 5 25 | " | .. | 4 | 2⅜ | 7 75 | " | .. | 6 | 2⅜ |
| 5 30 | " | .. | 4 | 2⅞ | 7 80 | " | .. | 6 | 2⅞ |
| 5 40 | " | .. | 4 | 3⅞ | 7 90 | " | .. | 6 | 3⅞ |
| 5 50 | " | .. | 4 | 4¾ | 8 .. | " | .. | 6 | 4¾ |
| 5 60 | " | .. | 4 | 5¾ | 8 10 | " | .. | 6 | 5¾ |
| 5 70 | " | .. | 4 | 6¾ | 8 20 | " | .. | 6 | 6¾ |
| 5 75 | " | .. | 4 | 7¼ | 8 25 | " | .. | 6 | 7¼ |
| 5 80 | " | .. | 4 | 7⅝ | 8 30 | " | .. | 6 | 7⅝ |
| 5 90 | " | .. | 4 | 8⅝ | 8 40 | " | .. | 6 | 8⅝ |
| 6 .. | " | .. | 4 | 9⅝ | 8 50 | " | .. | 6 | 9⅝ |
| 6 10 | " | .. | 4 | 10½ | 8 60 | " | .. | 6 | 10½ |
| 6 20 | " | .. | 4 | 11½ | 8 70 | " | .. | 6 | 11½ |
| **6 25** | " | .. | **5** | .. | **8 75** | " | .. | **7** | .. |
| 6 30 | " | .. | 5 | ..½ | 8 80 | " | .. | 7 | ..½ |

| Fr. Cts. | | £ | s. | d. | Fr. Cts. | | £ | s. | d. |
|---|---|---|---|---|---|---|---|---|---|
| 8 90 | = | .. | 7 | 1½ | 21 .. | = | .. | 16 | 9½ |
| 9 .. | " | .. | 7 | 2⅜ | 21 25 | " | .. | 17 | .. |
| 9 10 | " | .. | 7 | 3⅜ | 22 .. | " | .. | 17 | 7¼ |
| 9 20 | " | .. | 7 | 4⅜ | 22 50 | " | .. | 18 | .. |
| 9 25 | " | .. | 7 | 4¾ | 23 .. | " | .. | 18 | 4¾ |
| 9 30 | " | .. | 7 | 5¼ | 23 75 | " | .. | 19 | .. |
| 9 40 | " | .. | 7 | 6¼ | 24 .. | " | .. | 19 | 2½ |
| 9 50 | " | .. | 7 | 7⅛ | **25** .. | " | **1** | .. | .. |
| 9 60 | " | .. | 7 | 8⅛ | 26 .. | " | 1 | .. | 9½ |
| 9 70 | " | .. | 7 | 9⅛ | 27 .. | " | 1 | 1 | 7¼ |
| 9 75 | " | .. | 7 | 9⅝ | 28 .. | " | 1 | 2 | 4¾ |
| 9 80 | " | .. | 7 | 10⅛ | 29 .. | " | 1 | 3 | 2½ |
| 9 90 | " | .. | 7 | 11 | 30 .. | " | 1 | 4 | .. |
| **10** .. | " | .. | **8** | .. | 31 .. | " | 1 | 4 | 9½ |
| 11 .. | " | .. | 8 | 9½ | 32 .. | " | 1 | 5 | 7¼ |
| **11 25** | " | .. | **9** | .. | 33 .. | " | 1 | 6 | 4¾ |
| 12 .. | " | .. | 9 | 7¼ | 34 .. | " | 1 | 7 | 2½ |
| **12 50** | " | .. | **10** | .. | 35 .. | " | 1 | 8 | .. |
| 13 .. | " | .. | 10 | 4¾ | 36 .. | " | 1 | 8 | 9½ |
| 13 75 | " | .. | 11 | .. | 37 .. | " | 1 | 9 | 7¼ |
| 14 .. | | .. | 11 | 2½ | 38 .. | " | 1 | 10 | 4¾ |
| 15 .. | " | .. | 12 | .. | 39 .. | " | 1 | 11 | 2½ |
| 16 .. | " | .. | 12 | 9½ | 40 .. | " | 1 | 12 | .. |
| 16 25 | " | .. | 13 | .. | 41 .. | " | 1 | 12 | 9½ |
| 17 .. | " | .. | 13 | 7¼ | 42 .. | " | 1 | 13 | 7¼ |
| 17 50 | " | .. | 14 | .. | 43 .. | " | 1 | 14 | 4¾ |
| 18 .. | " | .. | 14 | 4¾ | 44 .. | " | 1 | 15 | 2½ |
| **18 75** | " | .. | **15** | .. | 45 .. | " | 1 | 16 | .. |
| .) .. | " | .. | 15 | 2½ | 46 .. | " | 1 | 16 | 9½ |
| 20 .. | " | .. | 16 | .. | 47 .. | " | 1 | 17 | 7¼ |

| Fr. | | £ | s. | d. | Fr. | | £ | s. | d. |
|---|---|---|---|---|---|---|---|---|---|
| 48 | = | 1 | 18 | 4¾ | 78 | = | 3 | 2 | 4¾ |
| 49 | " | 1 | 19 | 2½ | 79 | " | 3 | 3 | 2½ |
| **50** | " | **2** | .. | .. | 80 | " | 3 | 4 | .. |
| 51 | " | 2 | .. | 9½ | 81 | " | 3 | 4 | 9½ |
| 52 | " | 2 | 1 | 7¼ | 82 | " | 3 | 5 | 7¼ |
| 53 | " | 2 | 2 | 4¾ | 83 | " | 3 | 6 | 4¾ |
| 54 | " | 2 | 3 | 2¼ | 84 | " | 3 | 7 | 2½ |
| 55 | " | 2 | 4 | .. | 85 | " | 3 | 8 | .. |
| 56 | " | 2 | 4 | 9½ | 86 | " | 3 | 8 | 9½ |
| 57 | " | 2 | 5 | 7¼ | 87 | " | 3 | 9 | 7¼ |
| 58 | " | 2 | 6 | 4¾ | 88 | " | 3 | 10 | 4¾ |
| 59 | " | 2 | 7 | 2½ | 89 | " | 3 | 11 | 2½ |
| 60 | " | 2 | 8 | .. | 90 | " | 3 | 12 | .. |
| 61 | " | 2 | 8 | 9½ | 91 | " | 3 | 12 | 9½ |
| 62 | " | 2 | 9 | 7¼ | 92 | " | 3 | 13 | 7¼ |
| 63 | " | 2 | 10 | 4¾ | 93 | " | 3 | 14 | 4¾ |
| 64 | " | 2 | 11 | 2½ | 94 | " | 3 | 15 | 2½ |
| 65 | " | 2 | 12 | .. | 95 | " | 3 | 16 | .. |
| 66 | " | 2 | 12 | 9½ | 96 | " | 3 | 16 | 9½ |
| 67 | " | 2 | 13 | 7¼ | 97 | " | 3 | 17 | 7¼ |
| 68 | " | 2 | 14 | 4¾ | 98 | " | 3 | 18 | 4¾ |
| 69 | " | 2 | 15 | 2½ | 99 | " | 3 | 19 | 2½ |
| 70 | " | 2 | 16 | .. | **100** | " | **4** | .. | .. |
| 71 | " | 2 | 16 | 9½ | 150 | " | 6 | .. | .. |
| 72 | " | 2 | 17 | 7¼ | 200 | " | 8 | .. | .. |
| 73 | " | 2 | 18 | 4¾ | 250 | " | 10 | .. | .. |
| 74 | " | 2 | 19 | 2½ | 300 | " | 12 | .. | .. |
| **75** | " | **3** | .. | .. | 350 | " | 14 | .. | .. |
| 76 | " | 3 | .. | 9½ | 400 | " | 16 | .. | .. |
| 77 | " | 3 | 1 | 7¼ | 450 | " | 18 | .. | .. |

| Fr. | | £ | s. | d. | Fr. | | £ | s. | d. |
|---|---|---|---|---|---|---|---|---|---|
| 500 | = | 20 | .. | .. | 3500 | = | 140 | .. | .. |
| 550 | " | 22 | .. | .. | 4000 | " | 160 | .. | .. |
| 600 | " | 24 | .. | .. | 4500 | " | 180 | .. | .. |
| 650 | " | 26 | .. | .. | 5000 | " | 200 | .. | .. |
| 700 | " | 28 | .. | .. | 5500 | " | 220 | .. | .. |
| 750 | " | 30 | .. | .. | 6000 | " | 240 | .. | .. |
| 800 | " | 32 | .. | .. | 6500 | " | 260 | .. | |
| 850 | " | 34 | .. | .. | 7000 | " | 280 | .. | |
| 900 | " | 36 | .. | .. | 7500 | " | 300 | .. | .. |
| 950 | " | 38 | .. | .. | 8000 | " | 320 | .. | .. |
| 1000 | " | 40 | .. | .. | 8500 | " | 340 | .. | |
| 1500 | " | 60 | .. | .. | 9000 | " | 360 | .. | |
| 2000 | " | 80 | .. | .. | 9500 | " | 380 | | .. |
| 2500 | " | 100 | .. | .. | 10000 | " | 400 | | .. |
| 3000 | " | 120 | .. | .. | 20000 | " | 800 | .. | .. |

www.ingramcontent.com/pod-product-compliance
Lightning Source LLC
Chambersburg PA
CBHW030536270326
41927CB00008B/1403